ALCHEMY RISING

THE GREEN BOOK

HELIOPHILUS

ALCHEMY RISING

THE GREEN BOOK

BIBLIOTHÈQUE ROUGE
MMXVII

ALCHEMY RISING: THE GREEN BOOK
was first published by Scarlet Imprint in 2015
in an edition of 735, comprising 666 clothbound
copies & 69 copies half-bound in grey leather.
The paperback edition is published in 2017
under the Bibliothèque Rouge banner.

Copyright © Heliophilus, 2015
Typesetting & design © Alkistis Dimech
Edited by Peter Grey and Paul Holman

Printed and bound in the United Kingdom
ISBN 978-1-912316-01-4

WWW.SCARLETIMPRINT.COM

For Gabriel Gray

VOCATUS ATQE
NON VOCATUS
DEUS ADERIT

Contents

ILLUSTRATIONS: OLIVER LIEBESKIND

ACKNOWLEDGEMENTS

With deepest of thanks I'd like to recognise all those who have made this work possible, inadvertently or not. Special thanks, in no particular order, goes to Galahad Clark for the inspiration; to my family, Dad, Amber and Todd, and to my Mum especially, for their patience and faith; to the late Richard Allen, and family, for the memories; to Richie Tong for his beautiful work; to Christian Schwetz, Elliott Stallion and the feathery one, Jade Smith: fly far, float home, thanks for helping with the photographs; to Michael Brisbane for my very well behaved woofer; to Jasmine Paul for 'Bitterley' philosophical debates; to Chris King-Turner for pirating his hedges and fields for the wild flowers and herbs; to the marvellous Geraldine Beskine for the introduction; and finally, with the profoundest of thanks, Gary and Mary Nottingham who showed me the way to the Royal Road and without whom this work would not have been written; great teachers, great friends.

I would also like to thank Peter Grey and Alkistis Dimech of Scarlet Imprint for helping to resurrect British Alchemy from its ashes, and also humbly recognise all those artists, past, present and those yet to come. Now is the accepted time.

Heliophilus

Preface

That which is looked upon by one generation as the apex of human knowledge is often considered an absurdity by the next, and that which is regarded as a superstition in one century, may form the basis of science for the next. — PARACELSUS

Between the two pillars of Hermetic philosophy, Astrology and Theurgy, a central post was said to hold the entire firmament of Hermetic thinking aloft and although this great column emerges from the earliest of times it is much maligned: divine, yet disgraced; proud, yet scorned; lost, but not forgotten. Here stands the once mighty science of Alchemy a crumbling edifice to Hermeticism that rose so high it promised to unlock the gates of heaven.

The Royal House of Alchemy has long since fallen. Her crown, sought by the wisest and greatest, bejewelled with diadems of wisdom and forged by the hand of Divinity, now lies buried in the gutter of modern science. To rescue it we must reach into our nethermost, for the depths from which we draw this noble Art cannot be fathomed by the plummet of a shallow reason.

Alchemy is the *Secreta Secretorum*, the Mystery of Mysteries; it is the greatest of mazes, for there are those who, having dared to enter this Hermetic labyrinth, failed, poisoned by a wrong turn; or who entering lost their path; or who, having found the Great Secret, were hunted all their days. Ours is a road less travelled, a path obscure and obscured; therefore, Gentle Philosopher, we shall need a guide.

I

"HEAL THYSELF"

Paracelsus

Disease itself is of Nature, Nature alone understands and knows disease, and Nature is also the sole medicine of disease. – PARACELSUS

We must remember the time of his birth, a time when plague doctors roamed the streets burning incense from hazel sticks or wore grotesquely beaked masks filled with sacred herbs; churches adorned themselves with garlands of angelica and rang their bells ceaselessly, whilst the first surgical procedure recorded in Europe was conducted by a hog-gelder. Sorcerers healed the rich, barbers bled the merchants, midwives tended obstetric patients and witches healed the poor, and into this extraordinary situation was born a most extraordinary character: Philippus Aureolus Theophrastus Bombastus von Hohenheim. Paracelsus, meaning *greater than Celsus*, was the name given to him by his father; Aurelius (or Aulus) Cornelius Celsus being a 1st century physician of great renown.

'He is surely one of the most fascinating figures of the Renaissance,' notes A. E. Waite. 'Arrogant before his enemies, humble before his art, full of child-like faith, investigating everything by the light of nature, bombastic, despairing, hopeful, infinitely curious, a man who saw deeply into the spirits of matter, and into the souls of men.'

His contemporaries condemned him, hounding him from place to place. They found him too caustic, too unfamiliar; his conclusions too dissimilar to their own. His biographer Franz Hartmann notes, 'He was, however, far superior in medical skill to all his colleagues, and performed apparently miraculous cures among many patients that had been pronounced incurable by the leading doctors – a fact that has been proved by Erasmus of Rotterdam, a most careful and scientific observer. Among such patients were not less than eighteen princes, on whom the best physicians had tried their arts and failed. In his thirty-third year

Philippus Theophrastus Paracelsus. Oil on wood, after an engraving by Augustin Hirschvogel, from 1540.

he was already an object of admiration for the laity, and an object of professional jealousy for the physicians. He also incurred the wrath of the latter by treating many of the poorer classes without pay, while the other physicians unrelentingly claimed their fees.'

Though vast tracks of his work are occult and obscure – the words, the terms, the veiled meanings and countless blinds – when he declares in his book *Concerning the Nature of Things* how to resurrect a plant from its ashes,[1] or that he has fathered a homunculus from human sperm and blood and raised it; or has restored an old man to perfect youth, or indeed, transmuted base metals into gold, he is not speaking hypothetically, but quite literally. Gessner, writing to Crato von Crafftheim, observed: 'They (Paracelsus's students and followers) are given to senseless astrology, geomancy, necromancy, and other forbidden arts. I myself suspect they are the last of the Druids, those of the ancient Celts who were instructed for several years in underground places by demons... Theophrastus has assuredly been an impious man and a sorcerer and has had intercourse with demons.'[2]

Paracelsus travelled extensively and finally at the end of his great wanderings we find him recording his experiences, the remnants of which make up the Geneva portfolios: most of the contents would have been dictated, much of it ridiculed, and much of it is missing. Jung notes: 'His writings are as turbulent as his life and his wanderings. His style is violently rhetorical. He always seems to be speaking importunately into someone's ear – someone who listens unwillingly, or against whose thick skin even the best arguments rebound.' He eventually met his demise at the age of fifty two. According to his enemies he was killed in a drunken brawl; his friends said he was thrown off a cliff by hirelings in the pay of the medical faculty.

Reports say that he died on the 24th of September 1541 in a small room of the White Horse Inn and that his body lies buried at the church of St. Sebastian. Notably St. Sebastian was considered a protector from the ravages of the plague, having been shot with arrows (sacred to Apollo) and returned to life. This is a final touch that Paracelsus himself would have approved of, in a life rich with symbolic meaning. Later, a German physician, having handled his skull, concluded that a fracture through the temporal bone could only have occurred while

1 See the chapter 'The Plant Phoenix.'
2 See C.G. Jung's *Alchemical Studies*, p.119.

he was alive and was large enough to cause his death. According to the account of the reading of his last will and testament, he did not die immediately, but lingered a while.

No matter how he is regarded – magician, alchemist, doctor, quack – we should remember his life was dedicated to the art of healing and the eradication of disease. 'Around this cardinal principle,' Carl Jung notes, 'were grouped all his experiences, all his knowledge, all his efforts.' Compassion, in our own age, is in short supply, but it was Paracelsus's driving force. 'Compassion,' he confides, 'is the physician's schoolmaster.' Philosophers who share this passion for compassion will be warmly welcomed by us and everything we have learned will be shared with those of a pure and kindly heart.

It is strange to think, that had he been born a hundred years later, he would have certainly been persecuted by the Inquisition, for his work touches on some of the more irresolute aspects of magic and alchemy and although his claims, at times, seem too incredible to bear, we should remember the words of Hartmann, who gently reminds us:

> If an individual, being a reasonable sceptic says that such a thing does not exist relative to his knowledge, then that individual would be denying the possible existence of anything of which he knew nothing, and therefore imply that he imagined himself to be in possession of all the knowledge that exists in the world, and therefore believe that nothing could exist of which he did not know.

One can not ignore these mysteries, nor can we ignore the vast, rambling, cryptic, indecipherable, and unrivalled body of writing Paracelsus has left us, for in them, and as his reputation attests, lie hidden the cures for the most dreadful diseases, persecutions like cancer, syphilis, tuberculosis, diabetes and psychological complaints unbested by modern medicine.

Yet between his denouncements of Galen and Avicenna, the scourging of the medical faculty and his scathing opinions of apothecaries (at times calling them *dirty ointment-vending quacks*) and sophists, that litter his work, we see an incredible mind beginning to form, wide-eyed with curiosity, hungry for knowledge, searching everywhere, questioning everything. We find him learning from the rudimentary and uneducated, searching out the wise folk who lived in hovels

Elixir of Calendula

All matter originates and exists only by virtue of a force. We must assume behind this force is the existence of a conscious intelligent mind. This Mind is the matrix of all matter.

— MAX PLANCK

outside villages and towns. Here in the most disrespectable of educational establishments, he comprehended the vast and almighty Laws of his world. 'I went in search of my art,' he confides, in the preface of the *Paragranum*, 'often incurring danger of life. I have not been ashamed to learn that which seemed useful to me from vagabonds, executioners, and barbers. We know that a lover will go a long way to meet the woman he adores: how much more will the lover of wisdom be tempted to go on search of his divine mistress!'

At the age of sixteen he was sent to Basel to be tutored by the famous Abbot Johannes Trithemius of Spanheim, an adept in the sacred arts of astrology, magic and alchemy. Later he became a doctor in the great mines of the Hapsburgs, and then an army surgeon in the field and later still a bible salesman, not so he could spread the word of God, but in order to tour Europe in search of truth. Thence he travelled to India, where he was said to have been taken prisoner by the Tatars and lead before their Khan, whose son he later accompanied as doctor. But it was in Constantinople, among the Muslims, that he learned the secret of

"HEAL THYSELF"

the Philosopher's Stone and where he said, he had found men of true learning.

To Paracelsus the universe and the planets were living things, everywhere he found life and he declared emphatically that there was no vacuum in nature. He said that even in the four elements, there existed forms of life we cannot comprehend; those living in the principle of Fire he called Salamanders; in Water, Undines; in Air, Sylphs and in Earth, Gnomes.

He described the universe as being 'a manifestation of Will in motion,' and this causal All, the Absolute of the Pythagoreans, was but a fragmentation, a differentiation of vibrations proceeding from this singular Will. 'What fuels this Will?' questioned Paracelsus. 'Imagination,' he concluded, for even at the heart of the word we find *magi*. Imagination is the probability factor of our modern quantum theorists, a philosophy best summarised by the German philosopher Hegel when he writes: 'All things have their commencement in pure being, which is merely an intermediary thought.' 'What are phantasms, and what reality,' taunts Mephisto, 'where ends the man and begins the dream?'

To the ancient philosophers it is this Dream, this Thought, this Imagination that directs the Will. The Will then becomes the instrument or tool of the Imagination and when Will moves or causes Motion, the effect is Force and when the Motion of Will is exhausted in the release of Force, the result is Matter.

Will, Motion and Matter are therefore conditions of each other, and since Matter is a condition owing to a principle higher than itself, it is capable of being reabsorbed into that which is superior to itself.

On a macrocosmic level the imagination, or spirit, is the superior causal principle of matter or form, and when matter arises to meet spirit descending, we find the creation of three philosophical principles; body, soul and spirit.

Many traditions have similar trinities. In Christianity, the Father is the source eternal, the Son is the Word or Logos incarnate, the Holy Ghost is the light of the Father shining through the Son – it is that which comes from the centre, reaches the periphery and manifests as the 'Spirit of Truth' as the visible natural world.[1] The Hindus use the names Brahma, Vishnu, Shiva; the Buddhists use Atma, Buddhi and Manas; the Greeks Zeus, Athena, and Apollo; the Scandi-

---

[1] Manly P. Hall in *Lectures on Ancient Philosophy* observes: 'God as the Father impregnates SPACE with his seed; God as the Mother receives this seed into herself and protects it though the ages necessary for its unfoldement; and God as the Child is himself the seed which as God the Father he sowed.'

Plant mineral salts having been washed, filtered & gently dried. This process is known as solve et coagula in alchemy.

navian and Germanic tribes, Odin, Vili and Ve, whilst even atheists agree with cause, matter and energy.

'Anyone,' writes Albert Einstein to Phyllis Wright in 1936,[1] 'who becomes seriously involved in the pursuit of Science becomes convinced that there is a spirit manifest in the laws of the universe, a spirit vastly superior to that of man.' As we penetrate further into these trinities we will see they are merely aspects or personifications of this Causal Spirit.

In alchemy, we call this trinity Salt, Sulphur and Mercury. Sulphur represents the spiritual or Will factor; Salt is the body, representing the material factor or that which is further away from activity; Mercury unifies these polarities and represents both force and motion; motion being either the means by which one thing moves from one place to another, or by which a 'condition' or 'quality' can advance or retire from its existing state. The process by which matter is

1 See Max Jammer, *Einstein & Religion: Physics and Theology,* 1999; and Alice Caparice, *Dear Professor Einstein: Letters to and from Children,* 2002.

reabsorbed or retires into a state higher than itself Paracelsus called death. To us death is a total cessation of life and the decomposition of the body. To Paracelsus the death of the body was only the unshackling of form, which is just an illusionary compound, a by-product of universal law and therefore the body has no existence independent of an inner life/light principle. 'What is death?' he asked. 'It is that which takes the life away from us. It is the separation of the immortal from the mortal part. It is also that which awakens us and returns to us that which it has taken away.'

In *Isis Unveiled* Madame Blavatsky takes up the point: '*What, then is produced from death?* inquired Socrates of Cebes. *Life!* was the reply (Plato, *Phaedo* 71 D). *Can the soul, since it is immortal, be anything else other than imperishable?* (Plato, *Phaedo* 106 B) *The seed cannot develop unless it is part consumed*, says Professor Lecomte. *It is not quickened unless it die*, says St. Paul (1 *Corinthians* 15:36).'[2]

An example might help us illustrate the issue more clearly. Let us take the herb St. John's Wort. Only when we cut the herb and it 'dies' can we expect to capture its soul (essential oil/sulphur). Through fermentation it releases its spirit (alcohol/mercury) and only when the body of the plant is calcinated and washed can we extract the water soluble salts (mineral salt/body). Now who is to say that the plant is dead? The fact that any spagyrical or alchemical product has a dramatic effect on the body would suggest that it is not dead. Indeed, death only occurs when the body can no longer assimilate this life energy. An alchemical preparation is an exalted form of this life energy; indeed it is the magnet by which we create a focus within the body to attract the vitality surrounding us. This energy is the Character behind the Form. Paracelsus called this life giving principle of light many names, Azoth being one, the *mysterium magnum* being another. Through it and by it, man had the ability to fulfil his divine potential; firstly by the path of knowledge, which is trial and error, and secondly, through the light of inner knowing, or intuition, which in the animal kingdom is called instinct.

Eliphas Lévi referred to this eternal light as the fifth essence or quintessence: 'Light,' he writes in *The History of Magic*, 'that creative agent, the vibrations of which are the movement and life of all things; light, latent in the universal ether radiating about absorbing centres, which, being saturated thereby, project movement and life in their turn, so forming creative currents; light astralised in the

2 Blavatsky, *Isis Unveiled*. 1877.

Extracting Paracelsus's First Entity of Melissa. Note the menstruum has separated into three layers.

stars, animalised in animals, humanised in human beings; light, which vegetates all plants, glistens in metals, produces all forms of nature and equilibrates all by the laws of universal sympathy – this is the light which exhibits the phenomena of magnetism, divined by Paracelsus, which tinctures the blood being released from the air as it is inhaled and discharged by the hermetic bellows of the lungs.'

This light is Emerson's Over-Soul; Jung refers to it under the term *synchronicity*, a kind of internal presupposing of facts.[1] Freud couldn't get along with the idea at all, but to Paracelsus the path of knowledge or experience, without this intuitive, guiding light could never be found. Experience is not revealed

1 In *The Structure and Dynamics of the Psyche* Jung writes: 'This proof seems to me of great importance, since it would show that the rationally explicable unconscious … artificially, as it were, is only a top layer and that underneath is an absolute unconscious which has nothing to do with our personal experience. The absolute unconscious would then be a psychic activity which goes on independently of the conscious mind and is not dependant even on the upper layers of the unconscious, untouched – and perhaps untouchable – by personal experience.'

through things done, but by the reasons and understanding behind the things done. 'There are therefore,' confides our guide in his *Philosophia sagax*, 'two kinds of knowledge in this world: an eternal and a temporal. The eternal springs directly from the Light of the Holy Spirit, but the other directly from the Light of Nature.'

This 'Astral Light' is the harmonising and animating principle that quickens nature, it is the mediator between Soul and Form and for this reason, as Paracelsus contemplated, when we see forms through our exterior senses, we see things objectively, but when use our apperception, we will see the subjective internal light of things.

'It is the Light,' comments Walter Leslie Wilmshurst in his introduction to Atwood's *A Suggestive Enquiry*, 'that, anteriorly to that of the solar and stellar bodies and all other derivatives from it, originated at the primal *Fiat Lux*; "Light, rare, untellable; lighting the very light; beyond all signs, descriptions, languages"; the garment, or "glory" of God; the *lumen gloriæ* of the Scholastics. It is that Fire which Heraclitus rightly called "the father of all things."'

This is the Paternal Ens of life, Paracelsus's *Magnesia* (*Magnus ignis*). It is this astral soul, this spark or fire, created through and bound by the relationships of the planets and stars which forms man's soul. 'Man,' concludes Paracelsus, 'is therefore the quintessence of all the elements, and a son of the universe, or a copy in miniature of its soul and everything that exists or takes place in the universe exists and can take place in the constitution of Man.'

As Paracelsus observed, when things depart from this source of light they lose their perfect integration with this light; therefore that which is unconditioned becomes conditioned, that which is absolute and eternal becomes differentiated and mortal. He would have compared the problem to that of a candle; when you are sitting near to the candle you can read the book, but move away from the candle and you cannot read the book. Our guide is leading us into the field of Hermeticism, central to alchemical thinking; therefore let us pause and consider this most sublime meadow.

Rising in the east with the dawn of mind, it was said that the Emerald Tablet, recovered from a sarcophagus by Alexander the Great, had been written by the fabled Egyptian mystic Hermes Trismegistus. He was the Adept King who lived, according to Suidas, four hundred years before Moses. We will leave his disputed biography to conjecture, and instead turn to the works attributed to

True, without error, certain and most true;
that which is above is as that which is below,
and that which is below is as that which is
above, for performing the miracles of the One
Thing; and as all things were from one, by
the mediation of one, so all things arose from
this one thing by adaptation; the father of
it is the Sun, the mother of it is the Moon;
the wind carries it in its belly; the nurse
thereof is the Earth. This is the father of all
perfection, or consummation of the whole
world. The power of it is integral, if it be
turned into earth. Thou shalt separate the
earth from the fire, the subtle from the gross,
gently with much sagacity; it ascends from
earth to heaven, and again descends to earth;
and receives the strength of the superiors and
of the inferiors – so thou hast the glory of
the whole world; therefore let all obscurity
flee before thee. This is the strong fortitude
of all fortitudes, overcoming every subtle and
penetrating every solid thing. So the world
was created. Hence were all wonderful adap-
tations of which this is the manner. Therefore
am I called Thrice Great Hermes, having the
Three Parts of the philosophy of the whole
world. That which I have written is consum-
mated concerning the operation of the Sun.

him, namely the *Divine Pymander* and *Asclepius*, both of which deal with the question of regeneration; for the more practical aspect of alchemy, the *Tractatus aureus*, or the *Golden Treatise*; and opening, as tradition dictates, with the most famous of his writings, the *Tabula Smaragdina*, or *Emerald Tablet*.

This statement was meant to have been the most secret knowledge the world had ever known, for it says all things arise from within the forms out of which they are generated, all existing things have the seed within themselves for the perpetuation of their material kind and in the same manner, the greater is revealed through the lesser. The universe which mankind has progressed, has impressed itself upon him and through him, and in doing so man has become the epitome of its eternal laws:

> Everything is the product of the universal creative effort; the Macrocosm and the man (the Microcosm) are one. They are one constellation, one influence, one breath, one harmony, one time, one metal, one fruit.[1]

As the great celestial bodies wheel and spin through the heavens, great movements and patterns are formed, creating balance and unbalance, sympathy and antipathy through their dynamic relationship with one another. We see the same in the changing of the seasons. To the ancients, the Sun may have seemed to have died, his nature or quality diminishing with the passing of the seasons, but in truth, it is the Earth's position in relation to the Sun that changes. These fluxes of energy are due to these changing relationships rather than a change in the essential substance of the energy itself. Therefore, an organ becomes sick because it lacks the energy required to function normally. Herein lies the mystery of genetic diseases, in that we are not inheriting an hereditary illness, but the lack of vitality which results in the

---

1 Paracelsus, *Philosophia ad Athenienses*. We are reminded here of the writings of Plato, Hippocrates and Plotinus, where Nature is depicted as a living, conscious being engendered by a supreme Causal Truth.

degradation of the organ, which is repeated down the family line. By supplying the relevant organ with the necessary vitality to operate normally, or to remove any obstructions blocking this energy is the basis of Paracelsian healing. 'Each thing,' concludes Hartmann, 'from a sun down to a tumour in the body of an animal, constitutes a certain state of vibration of the one original essence and by applying a remedy which is in a near relation to a diseased organ (according to the quality of its spirit) we can induce a healthy action in that organ, and thus restore its normal condition.'

Perhaps Paracelsus's most striking conclusion with regard to restoring this lost vitality, or indeed transplanting sickness from one body to another, was his doctrine on the law of sympathy. There is a relationship between the thing quickening and the thing quickened. Since the same laws of existence are imprinted and inherent in our constitution we have a sympathetic relationship with everything born from those principles. Paracelsus referred to this ability in Man as the *magnes microcosmi*, for just as the lodestone attracts iron, so a magnet of a different sort can be prepared from a vital substance to attract vitality. In short, herbs, minerals and *mumia* (hair, blood, excrement et cetera) have a psychic gravity which, when brought into contact with things of an antipathetical or sympathetical nature and bound by imagination, will and faith, will duly affect the patient. In practical terms these were achieved through waxen figures, incantations and charms, psalms and excerpts from religious texts.

'Every organ in the human body,' affirms Paracelsus, 'is formed by the action of certain principles that exist in the universe, and the former attract the corresponding influences in the latter. Thus the heart is in sympathy with elements of the Sun, the gall bladder with Mars, the kidneys with Venus, the lungs with Mercury, the liver with Jupiter and the spleen with Saturn.' We see the same thinking in the *Upanishads*: 'Orange, blue, yellow, red, are not less in man's arteries than in the Sun. As a long highway passes between two villages one at either end, so the Sun's rays pass between this world and the world beyond. They flow from the Sun, enter into the arteries, flow back from the arteries, enter into the Sun.'

Examples of the law of sympathy are multifold. The following demonstrate how herbs, possessing a relationship to the intention, can be combined with a subject/patient or in the first example, a victim.

Take a peppercorn and rue and boil it with the hair of the subject, whilst repeating:

Non faccio bollire questi capelli,	*I do not boil the hair alone,*
Ma faccio bollire questa robba,	*But all these things together thrown,*
Unita a l'anima e it cuore	*With this heart and soul that he,*
Di quello che non possa più-vivere	*May perish and forever be*
E non mezzo all strege	*Only in witches' company!*
Tu ti debbi sempre trovare!	

To cure gout Alexander of Tralles recommended that henbane should be picked when the moon was in Aquarius or Pisces, whilst incanting the following charm:

> *I declare, I declare holy wort, to thee: I invite you to-morrow to the house of Fileas, to stop the rheum of the feet of M or N, and say, I invoke Thee, the great name of Jehovah, Sabaoth, the God who steadied the earth, and stayed the sea, the filler of flowing rivers, who dried up Lot's wife and made her a pillar of salt, take the breath of thy mother earth and her power, and dry the rheum of the feet or hands of N or M.*[1]

Another form of the law of sympathy, much discussed by Paracelsus, is the transference of disease to either human, plant or animal. It is a folk practice recorded throughout the British Isles. 'If,' says our guide, 'the Mumia be extracted from a diseased part of the person by a microcosmic magnet, and the magnet mixed with earth, and an herb is planted into it the Mumia in the magnet will be extracted by that plant, and lose its diseased matter, and react in a beneficial manner upon the Mumia contained in the body of the patient; but it is necessary that the selected plant should be one which bears the signature of the disease with which the patient is affected, so that it will attract the specific influence from the stars. In this way diseased elements may be magnetically extracted out of a person and inoculated into a plant.'

1 See Black, 1883.

The following are some recommended uses of plants, which I have edited from Paracelsus's own investigations.

In cases of skin disorders, mumia should be gathered from the diseased skin or ulcer and then planted under either Lady's thumb or Comfrey, which will then absorb the sickness into themselves.[2] One could also make a poultice of the fresh herb, leaving it in contact with the diseased part for 24 hours, whereupon the plant is buried in horse dung; as the plant rots the ulcer heals. In Brandenburg, if a person was afflicted with dizziness it was the norm to run naked after sunset three time through a field of flax, after which the 'flax will at once take the dizziness to itself.'[3]

In Black's *Folk Medicine* we read an account of a patient who had a 'most violent pain of the arm,' which was cured by the following means:

> ...they beat up red coral with oaken leaves, and having kept them on the part affected till suppuration, they did in the morning put this mixture into an hole bored with an augur in the root of an oak, respecting the east, and stopt up this hole with a peg, made of the same tree; from thenceforth the pain did altogether cease, and when they took out the amulet, immediately the torments returned sharper than before.

For swollen gums or sore teeth the root of groundsel or a splinter of blackthorn or willow is applied to the affected area and rubbed until it bleeds. The groundsel is buried in manure and left to rot, whereas the thorns are driven into the bark of the tree.

Paracelsus suggests that in cases of tuberculosis penny royal should be brought to bear on the disease and then planted with an orchid in the vicinity of an oak or cherry tree to cure the ailment. In the case of atrophy, where a limb or organ is wasting away, gather the mumia from the upper and lower joints of the diseased limb and again plant them under an oak or cherry tree. These operations should be repeated until the disease is transferred. An incantation, recorded at

---

2 Depending on whether the disease is of a hot or cold nature the herb would be placed in a stream (hot) or hung in a chimney (cold). For instance pulmonary diseases are considered cold and therefore the herb, having been brought into contact with the patient would have been hung and dried.

3 For more details see Thiselton-Dyer, T.F., 1889.

the trial of Bartie Paterson, 18th December 1607, to use whilst implanting disease into plants or animals runs thus:

> *To wend out of flesch and bane,*
> *In to sek and stane:*[1]
> *In the name of the Father, the sone and Haly Ghost.*

In Berkhampstead, in Hertfordshire, certain oak trees were famed for their ability to cure ague. A lock of the patient's hair was duly pegged to the oak and when firmly attached, the patient would jerk their head away, wrenching the lock of hair out and thereby transferring their ague to the tree.

Transference of disease was not only reserved for plants or animals. Transplanting disease to humans has a nefarious history, which is rarely discussed in polite society and therefore let us immediately investigate the possibility, partly because it is the most interesting and partly for the *modus operandi*.

In times past, a person with warts, or other diseases, would rub the infected area and wrap it in a piece of brightly coloured cloth, tie it in a ribbon and drop it on the way to church on a Sunday. Such packages were snares to attract foolhardy persons, who having opened the pouch and handling the contents would receive the disease. Witches place such 'magnets' under the doorsteps of their enemies to cause ill, rather than leaving the victim to chance.

Along the Welsh borders a friend of the patient, or the patient, would prepare a string of Rowan berries, knotted with fragments of the sick persons clothes and sometimes their hair. This necklace was hung on a low hanging branch along a path with the intention that anyone passing and touching the necklace would absorb the other person's disease.

On November 12th 1695, John Dougall was accused of prescribing a cure for a patient's convulsions by taking parings from the sick man's nails and hair from his eyebrows and the crown of his head which he 'bound up in a clout, with a halfpenny,' which was then placed on a path.

In Yorkshire we find the same formula being practiced, where once again persons with warts or some such skin malady rub the affected area with a cinder, tie it up in a little bag and drop it at the crossroads.

---

1 *Sek* or *sok* (earth) and *stane* (stone).

Diseases were also transplanted into animals and we see throughout history a number of such customs, from covering the affected area with a piece of bacon and then feeding it to a cat or a dog; to spitting in a toad's mouth to prevent tooth ache; in some areas this method was used to relieve whooping cough.[2] In certain parts of Devonshire and Scotland a child with chest infections would have a hair from his head placed inside some bread, which was then given to a dog. To cure ague (involuntary shivering), one would gather nine or eleven snails on a thread, the patient saying as each is threaded: *Here I leave my ague.* When they are threaded they should be frizzled over a fire, and as the snails disappear so will the ague.[3]

In 1822 a Toad doctor was known to travel through the country charging seven shillings (a week's wage) to cure the King's Evil, which he did by cutting the hind legs off a toad and hanging them round the neck of the sufferer in a silken bag. The toad was then released and as he waned and died, so the disease was said to perish. To cure quinsy, a throat infection, we are told to tie a live toad by its throat from a piece of string and hang it until the body drops from the head and thence to wear the string around your neck. Captured spiders tied up in a nutshell with silk are said to cure the ague. Antiquarian and alchemist Elias Ashmole writes, rather nonchalantly, 'I took, early in the morning, a good dose of elixir, and hung three spiders about my neck, and they drove my ague away. *Deo Gratias!*'

We are told in the witch trial of Agnes Sampson, that she tried to transfer an illness from Robert Kerr to a cat, but something went wrong and the disease was transferred to Douglas Dalkeith, 'who pined away and died thereof, while Robert Kerr "was maid haill."'[4] The transference of disease onto dead persons, called the Dead Stroke, was also much practiced:

> It was a common sight in London, not so many years ago, to see people who were evidently ill in mind as well as body being led up to the scaffold in Old Bailey so that the hand of a man just executed might be touched. Indeed,

2 'I assure you,' said an old Shropshire woman as she finished her account of the cure which she had often superintended, 'we used to hear the poor frog whooping and coughing, mortal bad, for days after and it would have made your heart ache to hear the poor creature coughing as it did about the garden.' First recorded in Cockayne, 1866.

3 See Black, 1883: 'Sympathy and Association of Ideas.'

4 See Dalyell, *Darker Superstitions of Scotland*. Waugh and Innes, Edinburgh 1834.

it became one of the sights, almost as much worth seeing, so it was considered, as the actual hanging; and it has been affirmed that at Northampton sufferers from goitre used to gather round the gallows when an execution took place, and wait their turn to ascend for the purpose of being healed. The executioner charged a small fee and then stroked the affected part with the dead man's hand.[1]

Another well documented sympathetic cure was the Weapon Salve, which the physician would apply to the weapon rather than the wound. Sir Kenelm Digby, Van Helmont, Paracelsus and Culpeper all attest to its wonderful properties, and throughout history we see recipes for such salves. In a letter written by Strauss to Digby, an account is given whereby Lord Gilbourne healed a carpenter, who had cut himself severely with an axe. 'The axe, bespattered with blood, was sent for, besmeared with an ointment, wrapped up warmly and carefully hung in a closet. The carpenter was immediately relieved and all went on well for some time, when, however the wound became exceedingly painful, and upon resorting to his lordship, it was ascertained that the axe had fallen from the nail by which it was suspended, and thereby become uncovered.'[2]

My own experience of weapon salves comes from encountering an old Welsh farmer who informed me that a cow he owned had cut herself deeply passing through a gate. Instead of calling for a vet, the farmer promptly adorned the gate with a salve and within days the wound had healed without infection.[3]

Jan Baptist van Helmont covers the subject in his treatise, *The Magnetick Cure of Wounds*,[4] but his enemies, enflamed by its heretical content, had him summoned before the Inquisition and he was briefly imprisoned. Paracelsus and Crollius, as to be expected, both cover the subject. I provide the latters' receipts for your interest:

---

1 See J.W. Wickwar, *Witchcraft and the Black Art.* Herbert Jenkins, London 1930.

2 See Thomas Joseph Pettigrew, *On the Superstitions connected with the History and Practice Of Medicine and Surgery.* J. Churchill, London 1844.

3 Whether he was speaking the truth or entirely inebriated, one can only guess. I'd like to believe the first, but suspect the latter.

4 Van Helmont, *A Ternary of Paradoxes: The Magnetick Cure of Wounds, Nativity of Tartar in Wine, Image of God in Man..* Translated by W. Charleton. J. Flesher for W. Lee, 1650.

Of the Moss grown on a humane skull[5] two ounces; Mumy half an ounce: Humane fat depurated two ounces: Oyl of Line seed twelve drachmes: Oyl of Roses, and Bole Armeniack, ana one ounce. Mix them and by frequent agitation incorporate them into an Unguent. Into which a splinter of wood, or the weapon stained with the patients blood, is to be immersed: the wound, during the time of its sanation, being defended from the injury of aër, bound closely up with clean swathes and mundified with the urine of the patient.[6]

Crollius's more detailed receipt follows thus:

5 Later alchemists gathered this moss from the skulls of dead animals, particularly those who have died a sudden death. Duly prepared road kill will suffice.
6 For further details see Van Helmont, 1650.

Of the Fat of a wild Boar,[1] and a Bear (the elder the Beasts the more efficacious their fat) ana four ounces. When these Fats have been, for the space of half an hour, decocted in good red wine, they are to be effused into pure, clean, cold water and the floating unctuous substance to be skimmed off with a convenient instrument, but the ponderous residence in the bottom to be ejected as excrementitious and useless. This done, (receipt) of the fairest Earthworms, frequently purified in white Wine, two sextaries: Let them be torrified in a well vernished earthen pipkin, in an Oven close luted, provided they burn not, and then be finely pulverated: Of this powder (receipt) one ounce: the brain of a wilde Boar exsiccated: red odoriferous Sanders: Mumy: the Bloodstone; ana one ounce. Finally, (receipt) of the mossy periwig of the skull of a man, destroyed by violent death, sheared off in the increase of the Moon, and her existence in a propitious house of Heaven, of *Venus* if possible, but on no condition of those two malevolent Planets, *Mars* and *Saturn*, the quantity of two Nutmegs. To all these decently pulverised and searced conjoin the foresaid fat and confuse them, according to the art of the Apothecary, into an incomparable Unguent, to be conserved with extraordinary diligence in a Glass or Gallipot, closely sealed up.

Sympathetic cures were capable of affecting a cure at a distance,[2] and we find many a recipe for removing 'moats' in the eye; and, in the Orkney Islands, we hear of a magician curing hæmorrhages: 'the name of the patient being sent to the charmer, he saith over some words, upon which the bloods instantly stopped.'[3] The incantation is missing, but a similar charm used in England for curing patients and which was in common currency, follows thus:

> *In the blood of Adam sin was taken*
> *In the blood of Christ it was all to shaken*
> *And by the same blood I do thee charge,*
> *That the blood of (NN) run no longer at large.*

1 Dead 'wood bears' (badgers) or 'hedge hogs' found on the side of the road would make more suitable alternatives.
2 Those interested in this subject will find the work of Edgar Cayce (1877-1945), an American Mystic capable of remote healing, worthy of interest.
3 See Rev. James Brand, *Brief Description of Orkney, Zetland, Pightland-Firth and Caithness.* 1701.

Further examples of sympathetic cures could easily fill an entire volume and so, for now, we must leave this field of Paracelsian healing and continue our inquiry into the Sacred Arts.

To Paracelsus medicine had no intrinsic nutritional value in itself, but only acted as carrier for the 'sympathetic vibrations' inherent within the medicant; nutrition being the means, or vehicle, by which energy is moved from one organism to another. Once harnessed this energy creates a magnetic focus, which draws a sympathetic vitality from the inexhaustible wellspring of light-like energy surrounding us. 'Every metal and every plant,' says he, 'possesses certain qualities that can attract corresponding planetary influences.' Crollius, a student of Paracelsus, comes to the same conclusions when he says that the 'earth or the receptacle'[4] should not be considered of value, but the *Astrum* or Hidden Heaven, bound to the medicine and to which the medicament owes its energy, is that which cures the disease.

> For the horse knoweth his manger, the birds their nest, the eagle the carkas and every medicine striveth to get to its place, and seeketh after that member that is like unto it by an inbred magnetick vertue which may well be called the inexpressible property, like to like, domesticks to domesticks naturally apply themselves, as the true philosophical Physitians have diligently observed by long experience the most undoubted rule of all.[5]

In making these conclusions, Paracelsus writes: 'If, for instance, a woman is deficient in the element of Mars, and consequently suffers from poverty of the blood, and want of nervous strength (anaemia), we may give her iron, because the astral elements of iron correspond to the astral elements represented by Mars and will attract them as a magnet attracts iron. But we should choose a plant which contains iron in an etherialised state, which is preferable to that of metallic iron.[6] In a case of dropsy it would be exceedingly injurious to give any remedy that would help to attract the evil influences of the moon; but the sun is opposed to the moon, and those remedies which attract the astral essences of the sun will counteract those of the moon, and thereby the cause of dropsy can

4 By which he means the medicine itself.
5 Crollius, Oswald, *Philosophy Reformed*, 1657.
6 Hartmann's footnote reads: *For instance, elder-berries (Sambucas).*

RUPA
*The physical form, the container
of all the other principles*

PRANA
The breath or vital life principle

LINGA SHARIRA
*The astral body, the ethereal image
or counterpart of the physical body*

KAMA RUPA
*The animal soul, the source of our
material mortal desires and passions*

MANAS
*Reason, intelligence, mind. It is from
manas, the thinker, that we derive
the word man*

BUDDHI
*The spiritual soul the container that
sheathes the pure & universal spirit*

ATMA
Pure and absolute spirit

*Paracelsus makes very similar
classifications for the seven aspects
of man's constitution, see opposite.*

be removed. The same mode of reasoning may be applied in all other astralic diseases.'[1]

Man gets sick because he lacks perfect unity in all his parts; he is a compound and since, as Francis Bacon confides, all compounds must dissolve, that which makes up man's parts must also decompose. The extraordinary longevity we hear being reached by the patriarchs of the Bible and the yogis of the East is fully realisable by man. 'We should live longer,' declares Sir Oliver Lodge. 'Death does not seem essential to an organism. We are secreting poisons, but if they are taken away and our bodies kept clean, there is no reason we should die.'[2] 'Did not,' cries John French indignantly, 'Artefius by the help of this medicine live to 1000 years?' 'But then,' mutters Ashmole, 'Incredulity was given to the world as punishment.'

We have the potential within ourselves to achieve incredible life spans in perfect health, but 'a house divided against itself will fall' and until Man understands what makes his *entire* constitution, his health will continue to fail. The ancients knew the roots of health were not to be found in the freedom from disease, but rather freedom from the cause of disease. But as long as modern science continues to examine Man's outer shell, his kernel, rather than the inner man, science will continue to fail us. 'That which we see is only the receptacle,' states Paracelsus, 'the true element is a spirit of life and grows in all things.'

Let us, therefore, think of ourselves in the same manner as those ancient priest healers and mystics, like the ancient siddhars of India who compared Man to the Lotus flower, which living in water draws the energy from the earth, whilst ever striving for that ineffable solar light from which it unfolds its entire potential. They split this single ray of consciousness, dividing Man's nature into seven archetypes.

The Qabalah, to which Paracelsus, like many alchemists, was deeply indebted, explores these classifications minutely and since the Qabalah is the road map to the soul we shall pause to consider this ancient philosophy.

'Magic,' teaches our guide, 'indeed is an art and faculty whereby the elementary bodies, their fruits, properties, virtues and hidden operations are comprehended. But the cabala, by a subtle understanding of the Scriptures, seems to trace out the way to God for men, to show them how they may act with Him,

1 See the chapter on Medicine in Hartmann, 1896.
2 See Manly P. Hall, *Man: Grand Symbol of the Mysteries.*

and prophecy from Him; for the cabala is full of divine mysteries, even as Magic is full of natural secrets.'[3]

The Qabalah has been described as the Yoga of the West, the word *yoga* meaning *union*, and describes how the one came to be diffused through the many. 'The Deity,' according to the Qabalists, 'is one because it is infinite. It is triple because it is ever manifesting.'[4] Thus is revealed the most ancient of knowledge, containing in itself the very philosophy or wisdom of how spirit dissipates into matter. Since that which is above is like unto that which is below on a macrocosmic level, we see a hierarchy of law unfolding in the inner body of man, the microcosm. 'It is here that we find,' Atwood notes, 'the greatest mystery of all, in that not only should man have the means to perceive his true own nature, he can also effect it.'

The Qabalah describes the different phases of manifestation unfolding according to archetype. The ten glyphs or sephiroth (archetypal laws or energy) are, to use the language of the Rabbi, ten emanations, linked by twenty-two paths representing phases of subjective consciousness by which the soul unfolds its potentiality, just as an acorn becomes an oak tree. Each path mediates between two sephiroth and it is the relationship of the two, in context to the whole, which creates polarities that in turn are sympathetical or antipathetical to one another. Each sephirah cannot be considered singularly, for each has a fourfold nature which are ascribed to the four worlds: *Atziluth*, the world of Archetype, the sphere of Divinity; *Briah*, the world of Creation, or world of Thrones, Kursiya; *Yetzirah*, the world of Formation, the sphere of angelic beings; and *Assiah*, the world of Action, the sphere of Matter.

Dion Fortune in *The Mystical Qabalah* explains it thus: 'Each sephirah contains the potentiality of all that come after it in the scale of down flowing manifestation. Kether contains the rest of the sephiroth, nine in number; and Chockmah, the second, contains the potentialities of all its successors, eight in number. But in each sephirah only one aspect of manifestation is unfolded; the subsequent ones remain latent, and the preceding ones are received by reflection. Each sephirah, then is a pure form of existence in its essence; the influence of preceding phases of evolution is external to it, being reflected.'

3 A.E. Waite, *The Aura of the Philosophers*, vol I, chapter IV, 'The Hermetic and Alchemical Writings of Paracelsus.'
4 See Blavatsky, *Theosophy*, vol. 46, p.307.

CORPUS
Or the elementary body (Limbus)

MUMIA
Or ethereal body; the vehicle of life (Evestrum)

ARCHÆUS
The essence of life, the Spiritus Mundi in Nature, the Spiritus Vitae in man.

SIDEREAL BODY
Composed of the influences of the 'stars.'

ADECH
The inner man or the thought-body, made of the flesh of Adam.

ALUECH
The spiritual body, made of the flesh of Christ; also called 'the man of the new Olympus.'

SPIRITUS
The universal Spirit.

Throughout his work he emphasises all physical bodies are of a twofold nature, terrestrial and celestial.

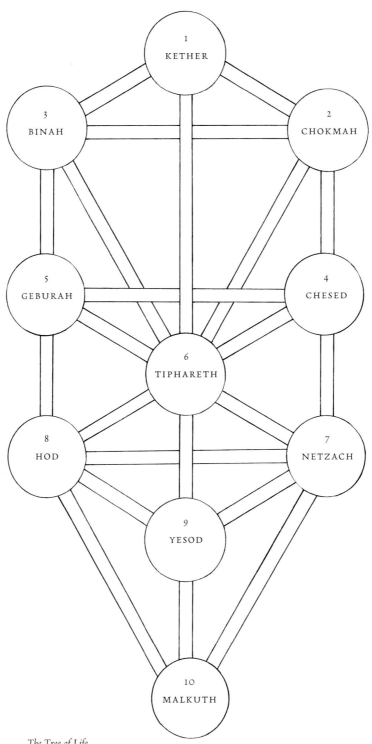

The Tree of Life

As Kether crystallises out of the Limitless Light it becomes the first great movement. In the words of Fortune: 'It is a condition of pure becoming, *Reshith ha-Gilgulim*, the First Swirlings; named the *Primum mobile* by the Alchemists.' From the overflowing of Kether, Chockmah comes forth, symbolically represented by the zodiac. 'The vibration,' states the *Secret Book of Dyzan*, 'sweeps along, touching with its swift wing the whole universe, and the germ that dwelleth in the darkness; the darkness that breathes over the slumbering water of life. Darkness radiates light, and light drops one solitary ray into the mother deep.' This is Uranus, Kether,[1] lord of the Titans and king of heaven whose wife was Gaia, the Earth Mother. Here is spirit and matter, polarities of that unconditioned essence, and the 'pull' or the space between these two was known by the Norse as the Ginnunga-gap. Here is the great cleft in space, the chasm of chasms, the great yawning gulf between the first morning and those depths, yet untouched by that glorious Light, no eye could fathom. From this womb Kronos was born for Kronos is Time, the royal child of Heaven and Earth.

Time is then the measure of separateness between Spirit and Matter. It is the means by which we can differentiate between these two polarities. Kronos represents the first beginnings of substantiality, the Great Formatter; the fruition, potential and completeness of all creation and yet we depict this Great Mother as Death, the scythe bearer. The symbolism is very revealing, for that which is born can die and that which is created must be uncreated and therefore Saturn, Time, Kronos, becomes the Reaper of Form, the 'all-devourer.'

The story unfolds when Kronos, discovering a prophecy that he would be deposed by one of his children, begins to eat them, but Rhea, his wife, wrapping a stone in swaddling saves their youngest child, Zeus. Now what principle or condition can withstand the ravenous appetite of Time? In Hindu mythology the condition arising from these three supernals, working together, is called Paramatman, the Primordial Over Soul, the 'Self beyond' or 'Supreme Soul of the World.' This is the great Olympian sky father, blazing forth as the root cause of consciousness. He is the source of Wisdom; he is intuition realising itself; he is Odin, the Great Wanderer, who tore out his eye for knowledge, but was prohibited from knowing whence he came or where his future lay. In the Hindu tradition this sphere is Thought, which in turn creates Mind and here we find

1 We say *could be* because our minds simply cannot get this close to deity; according to Plato, 'to define Deity, is to defile Deity.'

ATZILUTH
The World of Archetype, the sphere of Divinity

BRIAH
The World of Creation, or World of Thrones, Kursiya

YETZIRAH
The World of Formation, the sphere of angelic beings

ASSIAH
The World of Action, the sphere of Matter

Matter. The creator and destroyer. Saturn is the source of melancholy and sickness of the physical form.

JUPITER
The sphere of intuition, symbolised by the sacred number four. Jupiter is said to be the cause of ambition and pride.

LUNA, *the Moon*
She represents the astral body of man and the kingdom of his illusions and dreams.
She is Yesod, meaning foundation, and is called the Pure Intelligence since she 'rectifies' the preceding emanations. The moon is said to cause dreaming and fantasies.

Zeus, 'the eternal thinker thinking the non eternal thought,' and that thought is Creation.

To describe the individual attributes of each Sephirah would be too great a task for this work, so like a lightning flash we descend down the tree until we reach Malkuth, meaning kingdom, the realm of manifestation.

Binah	Saturn	Lead	Spleen
Chesed	Jupiter	Tin	Liver
Geburah	Mars	Iron	Gall
Tiphareth	Sun	Gold	Heart
Hod	Mercury	Quicksilver	Lungs
Netzach	Venus	Copper	Kidneys (reins)
Yesod	Moon	Silver	Brain

Paracelsus contradicts himself in places, using an entirely different set of correspondences. In his book *Concerning Degrees and Compositions in Alchemy* we find the following: 'Further, in the same way as they admit of a sevenfold division, the body also is subject to the same classification and they correspond one to another, so that the those things which are under the sun are appropriate to the heart, and these twofold; while those under the moon are, in like manner, appropriate to the brain, and that in either grade. Those things which are under Venus are heating to the reins; those things under Saturn strengthen the spleen; those which are under Mercury defend the liver; those under Jupiter have regard to the lungs; finally those subject to Mars are considered wholly adapted to the gall.' Whereas in his *Alchemy: The Third Column of Medicine* he affirms: 'For instance everything relating to the brain is led down to the brain by means of Luna. What relates to the spleen flows thither by means of Saturn; all that refers to the heart is carried by means of Sol. So, too, the kidneys are governed by Venus, the liver by Jupiter, the bile by Mars.' We have chosen the latter classifications for our work, but it is up to each individual alchemist to make their decision on the matter.

When the ancient Qabalists spoke of these planets they were referring to the spiritual principles represented by these celestial spheres and by so doing the Qabalah, says our guide, 'teaches of and foretells from the nature of things to come as well as of things present, since its operation consists in knowing the inner constitution of all creatures, of celestial as well as terrestrial bodies: which is latent within them; what are their occult virtues; for what they were originally designed, and with what properties they are endowed.'

Since that which is above is like unto that which is below we see the same archetypal characteristics reflected in the plant world. A teaching clarified by Culpeper in his *Complete Herbal*, where he illustrates how the government and virtues of certain herbs correspond to the dominion of the seven celestial spheres and the sympathetic relationship they have to our vital organs. In the third part we have included an Herbarium, which echoes these signatures with descriptions of the properties of these herbs. Alchemy is the only art that aims to capture and actuate these vibrations; she is the means by which we separate the pure from the impure, capturing and exalting these energies, which will improve health and awaken inner faculties within our physical body. We have chosen not to elaborate on the spiritual roots of alchemy, nor the impact alchemically prepared products might have. We allow Nature to speak for herself on such matters and gently remind the reader that these products are very subtle and penetrating; see the chapter entitled 'Consummation' in the present volume. So to conclude, 'If I have manna in my consti-

SOL, the Sun
He is our king, our gold. As we have seen there is more than one sun or light of nature, for when the ancients discuss the Sun or Sol, they mean to describe the ineffable rays of pure being; the light of the physical sun and the inner light of man. His name in the Hebrew tradition is Tiphareth, Beauty, and is called the Meditating Intelligence or the Lesser Countenance: both the universe and the heart centre in man are equilibrated by this principle and that which is higher is transmuted into the lower and that which is lower is transmuted into the higher. He is the cauldron where force and form meet and for this reason he has been considered the Christ centre, the sacrificed God. The sun is the source of wisdom.

MARS
Force, drive, Kama, courage. He represents the animal element in man, the throne of desire and the ego. He is called the 'Radical intelligence' and his title is 'Strength.' Mars causes fiery tempers.

MERCURY
Hod is the Eighth of the First, the principle of intelligence manifesting through mind. Called the 'Absolute Intelligence,' his virtue is honesty and through him form is ensouled, for he is the mediator, the power of nature in equilibrium, the messenger between the gods (spirit) and man (matter) or the supernal intelligence coagulating into the primordial. It is for these reasons the Alchemists employ him in their symbolism. Mercury is said to be the root of intelligence. Throughout ancient literature and art we find Mercury (Roman), Hermes (Greek), Thoth (Egyptian) and Nebo (Chaldean), Lord of the Writing Tablet, as representatives of the single principle that is Mind.

VENUS
The principle of purity and Love which is the means by which opposites can be joined in unity. Divine love and self knowledge is also represented by Netzach, for our Lady means Victory and when, in loving embrace, she couples with Mercury we find wisdom.

tution,' Paracelsus proclaims, 'I can attract manna from heaven. Melissa is not only in the garden, but also in the air and in heaven. Saturn is not only in the sky, but also deep in the earth and the ocean. What is Venus but the Artemisia that grows in your garden? What is iron, but Mars? That is to say Venus and Artemisia are both the products of the same essence, and Mars and iron are both manifestations of the same cause. What is the human body but a constellation of the same powers that formed the stars in the sky? He who knows what iron is, knows the attributes of Mars. He who knows what Mars is knows the qualities of iron. What would become of your heart if there was no sun in the universe? What would be the use of your *vasa spermatica* if there were no Venus? To grasp the invisible elements, to attract them by their material correspondences; to control; purify and transform them by the living power of the Spirit – this is true Alchemy.'

Thus we see a single radiating source of energy, dissipating into a septenary of archetypes which are the creative force behind the mundane world, and as we have said, when we find spirit descending and form ascending we find the creation of three essential principles: soul, spirit and body.

Sulphur, soul, is the symbol of the will, the Fire of the alchemists; spirit or Mercury is the mediator, the messenger between the soul and the body or salt. Salt represents the matrix, or that which is furthest removed from the soul, and into which the elements and spirit are forged and yet the principles of salt are bound and owing entirely to conditions higher than itself. Death and Art are the means by which we can exalt it, so it can be refined from its materiality. They are the first steps to regeneration, by which a thing can be raised from its materiality and be resurrected, like a phoenix rising from its ashes.

With these words we leave our theoretical enquiry, for the greatest gate of occult philosophy now stands before us.

Beginning the Quintessence of Lady's Mantle

II

ORA ET LABORA

The Work

Spagyrics essentially deals with the healing of the body and Alchemy with the healing of the soul.
– JEAN DUBUIS

An alchemist works with nature, guiding her, never forcing her. To be a success-ful alchemist one must obey Nature's laws and observe her ways. Throughout the alchemical corpus we see this repeated, but I believe the late Jean Dubuis, a leading light in the story of modern day alchemy, says there should be three ad-ages an alchemist and spagyricist should adhere to; thus, before contemplating any alchemical work, it is worth internalising his wise words:

· I accelerate the process of Nature by never stepping out of its rules.
· I remove the obstacles, which prevent Nature from acting spontaneously.
· I strive to help Nature in the work of universal reintegration.

An alchemist must have a place to work, his or her laboratory, into which only those initiated into the art should be allowed to enter. There are a number of reasons proposed for this, but I think the most relevant is that one is dealing with highly actuated substances, whose vibrations are acutely attuned to their environment and the person handling them. Allowing strangers into your work-ing laboratory would be like allowing someone to lick your spoon before you used it. One jests, but many adepts wholly agree with the ancients that the na-ture of the alchemist and their level of spiritual development can encumber the work and therefore purity of heart and virtue of soul are considered as being prerequisites to success.

The Fellows

'When this work is developed,' Dubuis adds, 'it will change our concept of Energy and Life. Alchemy is transmutation, revolution, renewal, and evolution both on the physical and spiritual levels. The only obstacle is the lack of a certain quality of consciousness.'

In my experience, being at peace before starting any work has tremendous benefits; it calms the mind and allows the imagination to organise the work, formulating and understanding it before the hands can take the lead.

Perhaps the most famous axiom relating to our work, and to this day still echoed by many modern philosophers, is *ora et labora*, (pray and work); indeed, our *labora-t-ory* is a synthesis of this. This is your studio and whether it is a small shed in the back of your garden or a fully equipped laboratory, one should treat this space with the deepest reverence; it is a place where the alchemist and the divine laws of nature come together.

The Fellows are also incredibly important. Glassware is an asset, the collection of flasks, retorts and alembics will be your tools. Heating mantles are ideal to maintain regular heat, but a simple electric hob will work just as well. In the later works a small crucible furnace or athanor will be essential for prolonged calcinations and the work on metals, but a crucible buried in the embers of a fire will do fine for most herbal preparations. Perhaps the most important piece of equipment, and one I value highly, is an incubator. Be creative; I made mine from a polystyrene box and a heating mat which is simple, effective and inexpensive.

Our art is like no other, the most secret and most ancient of arts, yet one of the simplest in operation; as Mary Anne Atwood once said:

> All that is performed in the proto-chemic artifice may be comprehended in three terms – solution, sublimation and fixation (coagulation). Solution dissolves and liquefies the included spirit; sublimation volatises and washes it; and after calcination there is a reunion into a more permanent form of being.

The way is simple, but the path is hard; some will strive and never succeed, whilst others will find they are born to the work. Ours is also a spiritual tradition and the seeker who takes a comparative approach to religion and philosophy and applies them to their greater understanding, will reap more rewards than one who is entrenched in dogma.

I should perhaps add an apology at this point, for my work is not complete. I am also no chemist or scientist and still stand in childish wonder at what happens in my retorts and flasks. I am a simple alchemist, following and probing the way that others have laid before me, with the pure hope that what these great teachers once taught can be used today; for if ever there was time their knowledge was needed, it is now.

... consider the ground of this Hermetic Mystery, and whether there be still an entrance open, as there was once said to be, to the shut palaces of Mind. Let us descend into ourselves, and believe in ourselves if we be able, that that which we are is worthy our investigation; and we may discover, as we proceed, by their traditional light unfolding it, that the wisdom of the ancients was not the outward, adventitious acquisition or vain display which it has been supposed to be, but a very real, substantial and attainable good.

– M. A. ATWOOD

Rectified Spirit of wine (alcohol) is the universal menstruum of the plant kingdom. It readily absorbs and carries the mercurial vibrations of the plant. We call it Mercury (Hermes being the messenger god) for it is the mediator between Spirit, Sulphur (the plant's essential oil) and the Body, (the plant's mineral salts); without it soul and body would not unite.

The Three Essentials

The Spirit is the Secret that has been hidden since the beginning of things.   – PARACELSUS

'Every thing,' says Paracelsus, 'which is generated and produced of its elements is divided into three, namely, into Salt, Sulphur and Mercury. Out of these a conjunction takes place, which constitutes one body and an united essence. This does not concern the body in its outward aspect, but only the internal nature of the body. Its operation is threefold. One of these is the operation of Salt. This works by purging, cleansing, balsaming, and other ways, and rules over that which goes off in putrefaction. The second is the operation of Sulphur. Now, Sulphur either governs the excess which arises from the two others, or it is dissolved. The third is of Mercury, and it removes that which changes into consumption. Learn the form which is peculiar to these three. One is liquor, and this is the form of mercury; one is oiliness, which is the form of sulphur; one is alcali, and this is from salt. Mercury is without sulphur and salt; sulphur is devoid of salt and mercury; salt is without mercury or sulphur. In this manner each persists in its own potency.' We have purposely not discussed the Elements, Fire, Water, Air and Earth in any detail. These elements are the building blocks of form. We will discuss Hollandus's Quintessence in more detail, but for now, when alchemists speak of the Elements, they mean that which is of the nature of Fire is hot or burning, tthat which is of Water possesses aqueous or fluidic properties; that which is of Air is gaseous or vaporous; and, finally, that which is of Earth has solid or finite characteristics. Be careful of this blind.

Alchemy is the process by which we separate and recombine these essentials and it should be noted that every kingdom has its Mercury, its mediator and each is universal to that kingdom; in the plant kingdom it is alcohol, or as it is

known in alchemical writing 'spirit of common wine' or *spiritus vinus*. This can either be fermented from the body after the extraction of the sulphur or rectified from another source, red wine or brandy being the most suitable as they come from the grape and the vine is a solar plant. 'Alcohol,' says Jean Dubuis, 'is the cloak of Mercury in t he vegetable realm.'[1] Fermenting t he herb and then rectifying t he spirit is called the Long Path. We have not included instructions for fermenting plant material, but rat her we have taken the Short Way, by which we take grape alcohol, red wine or brandy and distil.

We must remember that the Mercury in each kingdom, animal, vegetable and mineral, is universal to that kingdom. For example, I can use rectified grape alcohol to extract the essentials from any plant. The same goes for the mercury of metals; if we can find the universal mercury in the metal kingdom we have discovered what the ancients were desperate to conceal and this will be the aim of *The White Book*, our following volume on menstruums.

The sulphur or soul in the plant kingdom is the essential oil of our subject. It can be separated using a steam distillation setup, or alternatively gathered by immersing the herb in our alcohol, which will dissolve the mercurial vibrations of t he plant and t he plant's s ulphur. This is called an essen ce or tincture. It should be noted that there is a volatile sulphur and a fixed sulphur, the volatile is the essential oil and the fixed sulphur can be prepared and extracted in the same way as the plant salt.

1 Dubuis, J., *Spagyrics* Lesson 20, Vol. I, Triad Publishing 1987.

Having washed, filtered & dried the salts, repeat the operation until they are perfectly white. More often than not by the third cycle these salts will turn a bluish colour. Thus prepared, place them in a sheltered position during the run up to the full moon to deliquesce, dry and repeat.

Note carefully: when drying your salts watch your heat. Some salts will 'vitrify' or turn to glass at higher temperatures, which kills their philosophical nature.

'And the spirit of God moved upon the face of the waters.' See our chapter on the Plant Stone of Hollandus

Once we have extracted the tincture, the mercurial vibrations of the plant and the volatile sulphur, we then calcine the *caput mortuum* to an ash and wash the ashes in distilled water, filtering through organic coffee filters and evaporating the water to leave us with the plant's mineral salt. This process is called coagulation. Once we have separated the essentials we recombine them and allow them to circulate in an incubator.

We will learn more from application than from study and therefore let us turn our will to the work.

Tinctures

The primal matter introduces new youth into a man, just as a new herb springs forth from a new seed in a new summer and a new year.   – PARACELSUS

An essence or tincture contains the plant sulphur and the mercurial vibrations of the plant and is extracted by pouring rectified spirit of wine or brandy over the dried herb, leaving it to digest and then separating the two. A spagyrical tincture separates each essential and recombines them. Our first preparation will be a simple, but nevertheless effective product. For initiatory purposes it is our intention to create seven preparations, whether they be tinctures, elixirs, magisteries or first entities,[1] these will awaken and restore our vitality and should be seen as plant talismans, indeed for this purpose those familiar with the consecration and charging of talismans will do well to use these allies in ritual. Our first spagyrical tincture can be confected in a relatively short time, however the longer the herb is allowed to circulate the stronger the tincture becomes. As we progress we will exalt our products, which will have a subtle, if not profound, effect on our anatomy. One uses the term as Paracelsus would have used it, to describe our twofold constitution, which is both etheric and physical.

Frater Albertus, a leading light in the field, once described Alchemy as the art of 'raising up vibrations,'[2] and prolonged consumption of alchemically prepared products will open the psychic centres of the body, which may lead to an increase in awareness, more synchronicity or sensitivity as well as general well being. Let us approach the work.

---

1 These seven tinctures correspond to our energy centres, which in turn correspond to our vital organs.
2 Frater Albertus, 1974.

TINCTURE OF NETTLES

RECIPE

Dried Nettles 500 grms
Brandy 500ml
Coffee filters
Bottled water

Nettles are under the government of Mars and are a sovereign blood purifier. For those of you who have sciatica or arthritis, Paracelsus called these tartaric diseases, which are due to the build up of sediment around the joints, which in turn traps the nerves causing pain.

If you choose to pick your nettles then gather them on a waxing moon, as the rise and fall of energies in a plant rises and falls with the lunar tides, as do many other living things. Therefore we will pick them when their energies are high and their sap is up. Gather the whole herb, including the roots, and do not let them touch the ground. Once you have gathered them, dry them in a warm shady place.

When ready, place the nettles in a kilner jar and pour the brandy over them. For added security use cling-film over the mouth of the jar before fastening it shut and tucking it away in a warm dark spot, an airing cupboard would be ideal, but we suggest that one should eventually make an incubator with a thermostat.[1] This is why Paracelsus says 'our work starts in darkness and in death.'

Leave to digest for at least two weeks. In that time the brandy will have extracted the 'tincture'[2] (the mercurial vibrations and the sulphur) from the herb. Squeeze the dead plant, the *caput mortuum*, and place it in the pan and calcinate the plant to a grey or, better still, white ash. Gather these ashes and drop them in a glass and pour distilled water over them. The water will absorb the water soluble salts of the plant, filter the mixture into a glass beaker or pan and evaporate the water off gently. You'll notice a salt forming, the *Sal Salis* – Salt of Salts – which has a very sharp, penetrating taste. Gather these up and grind them before calcinating them again to a perfect whiteness. If you have an open fire, nestle the crucible or pot on the embers making sure the smoke is taken up the chimney; if not calcinate outside. The salts are ready when they have become white. By repeating the process, *solve et coagula*, we can make them blue. Wait for your salts to cool and then grind them with a pestle and mortar. Spread them thinly on a plate and take them outside in the evening to deliquesce, remembering to collect them before dawn.

1 A simple incubator can be made from a polystyrene box and a reptile heat mat attached to a thermostat.
2 Paracelsus refers to the tincture as the *essence*.

Our salts have become like a magnet, drawing the vitality out of the air. The moisture in the air, the dew, contains the philosophical fire of the alchemists, which will be absorbed into the plant salts and quicken your spagyrical tincture. Calcinate the salts gently, repeating the process so that the salts are saturated with our fire and finally add them to your clear tincture. Put all in a pelican and circulate for a philosophical month (40 days) at which point it will be ready for use.

Since this is a simple spagyrical preparation the dose should be no more than two tea spoons of tincture in a glass of water three times a day. However, this is just a rough guide and it all depends on what plant one starts with. Many of the herbs we find in our hedgerows are entirely beneficial with no side effects, but we strongly suggest that one should do some research or consult a professional herbalist where doubts arise.

All things are one tree, with one origin, one root, from one stalk. – PARACELSUS

Elixirs

If we know Nature we know Man, and if we know Man we know Nature.   – PARACELSUS

According to Jean Dubuis one of the differences between an alchemical preparation and a spagyrical preparation is the circulation of the final product. 'The word spagiry,' he confirms, 'comes from the Greek and means to separate and reunite. In the spagyrical process we separate the alchemical principles of Salt, Sulfur and Mercury and we can thus purify them separately. Sometimes, as much in the mineral as in the vegetable realm, we accomplish only one separation: the Salt on one side and the tincture on the other, that is the mix Sulfur/Mercury. Then, we reunite the two or three products and we obtain a liquid or solid, fixed or volatile elixir depending on the processes used. Now if these products are circulated or if the calcination of the salt is repeated, we enter into the alchemical domain, and this happens regardless of the realm to which the product treated belongs. The true difference between spagyrics and Alchemy lies in the fact that if spagyrics and Alchemy both purify the product, Alchemy in addition provokes its evolution.'[1]

Not surprisingly Paracelsus's definition is far more ambiguous in that he defines an elixir as a virtue rather than a process.

'For every elixir,' says he, 'is an inward preservative in its essence of that body which shall have taken it…we call this preservative an elixir, as if it were yeast, with which bread is fermented and digested by the body. Its virtue is to preserve the body in that state wherein it finds it,[2] and in that same vigour and essence. Since this is the nature of preservatives, namely, that they defend from corrup-

---

1 Dubuis, Jean, *Spagyrics* Lesson 26, Vol. II, Triad Publishing 1987.
2 By this definition an elixir can be used to preserve dead bodies.

a) Due to a greater surface area an alembic allows for a quicker distillation than a retort, which is better suited for smaller quantities and more precise distillations. For volatile substances the system will need to be hermetically sealed or you shall lose that which is most precious.

b) Distilling the spirit of wine; note the small globule of oil on the surface: this is the sulphur of wine.

tion, not in any way by purifying, but simply by preserving. The fact that they also take away diseases is due to the subtlety which they possess. So, then, they do not only preserve, but they also conserve.'[1] In this respect a quintessence can be reduced to an elixir due to its conserving properties.

Whereas a simple spagyrical tincture separates the pure from the impure, recombines each essential and then circulates them in a suitable vessel, an alchemically prepared product or elixir refines each principle before recohobating the tincture over the salt and distilling the tincture (the mercury/sulphur mix) over the body a number of times. This constant recohobation and distillation is referred to as 'letting the eagles fly' and opens up the pores of the salt/body, allowing them to volatise and pass over the receiver with the mercury. The result will be that we have volatised or 'spiritualised' the body or mineral salts, which can then enter the system more efficiently.

1 The Eighth Book of Archidoxies, 'Concerning Elixirs.'

The spagyrical tincture previously discussed is the first step into practical initiation[2] and is ideal for quick extractions when the need arises. However, an alchemical elixir will require us to take more time over the work, but in terms of creating a more refined and penetrating product it will be well worth the effort.

    The most important aspect of this lesson is the *modus operandi*, as it allows us to approach other kingdoms. Firstly, we shall consider what the author(s) of the *Collectanea Chemica* has to say on the matter:

> Take any herb which is potent in medicine, and either extract the tincture with spirit of wine, or distil in the common way; reserve the distilled water, or tincture, when separated from the fæces, for use. Then take the fæces or *Caput Mortuum* and calcine it to a calx. Grind this to powder. That done

c) The sulphur of wine has many curative properties, collect and keep aside.

d) 'Our work begins in darkness and in death.' We macerate the plant using 50% distilled water and 50% distilled spirit of wine and digest in an incubator.

---

2 'True initiation is repair, compensation for what various religions call the original fall from grace.' Dubuis, Lesson 28, *Spagyrics* Vol 11.

The clear distillate in the
receiver contains the mercurial vibrations of the plant
and the plant sulphur. The
dark plant soup in the retort
contains the fixed sulphur.

take the water, or tincture, and mix them together; distil again, and calcine,
forcing the moisture over by a retort, in a wary process, calcining and coho-
bating the spirit on the salt till it attains a perfect whiteness and oily nature,
like the finest alkali, commonly called Flemish. As your salt requires it in the
process, have in readiness more of the extracted tincture, or distilled spirit,
that you may not work it, viz., the salt, too dry; and yet proceed cautiously,
not adding too much of the moisture, so that the dealbation, or whitening,
may keep visibly heightening at every repetition of the process. Frequent
experiments may enable you to push it onto a redness, but a fine yellow
is the best of all; for this process tends, in its perfection at this period, to
a state of dryness, and must be managed with a strong fire. By following
these directions, you have here the two tinctures in the Vegetable Kingdom,
answering to the white and red tinctures in the mineral.[1]

We use this method regularly and it is our preferred means of confecting elixirs.

1 *Collectanea Chemica*, Ch. 11 'Of the Vegetable Tincture...' Vincent Stuart Ltd, London 1963, p.65.

ELIXIR OF HORSETAIL

We have chosen horsetail, which is under the rulership of Saturn; and we will aim to gather the herb on the planetary day and hour on a waxing moon. Having made supplications we will cut the herb cleanly and not allow it to touch the ground: this precedes the hanging and drying. These dried herbs can then be ground and preserved away from sunlight in air tight jars.

One of the most important ingredients an alchemist will need is a good supply of rectified Spirit of Wine, therefore take either strong red wine or brandy from the grape and pour it into a flask and attach to an alembic, which in turn is fastened to a receiver. The benefits of using an alembic is that it has a wider surface area than a retort and therefore quickens the distillation process. The alcohol will come over the receiver at 76°C, leaving the water, or phlegm, and plant faeces behind. Once we have the clear distillate that is our Spirit, we will need to rectify it again. But first we will need to remove the faeces from the retort and calcinate them to ashes. Once we have calcinated and washed the ashes, extracting the water soluble salts in the usual way,* we will deliquesce them until they liquefy. This process occurs under a waxing moon. The following morning we will dry them gently and then replace in the evening. By repeating the operation, *solve et coagula*, the wine salts will be charged with the 'astral fire.' Finally dry the salts, grind, and having placed the distilled spirit into a suitable retort, pour it over the salts, hermetically sealing the retort and receiver as we did at the beginning of the operation.

We then distil the spirit again, each time leaving a little of the liquid in the retort, which we pour into an evaporating dish and then calcinate before recohobating them over the spirit. By the third or fourth distillation you will notice globules of oil resting on the alcohol. This is the volatile sulphur of wine, and has many curative properties in itself, and therefore, once we reach the end of the distillation, place the liquid in a separating funnel, collecting and bottling the oil for later use. We now have a highly rectified vegetable mercury which we can use to extract the 'tincture' of any plant.

In addition to this we need distilled rainwater to wash, then coagulate, the plant salts. This is preferably gathered during a thunderstorm, but heavy showers or indeed dew are all ideal. Failing that, distilled spring water or distilled bottled water are both acceptable.

RECIPE

Herb
Spirit of Wine 250 ml
Distilled Rainwater
250 ml
Kilner Jar
Alembic
1 ltr Retort
1 ltr Receiver

* NOTE: *cover the beaker with tin foil, so as not to lose any volatised salts. Prick the foil with a pin.*

a) Gently evaporate the plant soup   *b) Place in crucible*

Place your horsetail in a kilner jar and pour 250 ml of rectified spirit of wine and 250ml of distilled water over the herb. Seal the jar and leave in an incubator or warm cupboard to digest for two weeks, shaking the jar every day. After two weeks squeeze the macerated herb dry and pour the greenish brown tincture back into the kilner jar before adding fresh herbs and returning the jar to the incubator. Refrigerate the dead body for later calcination.

When the liquor has been saturated, remove the jar, separate the dead plant material and pour the tincture into a flask and fit an alembic. Hermetically seal and gently distil the clear spirit, which will carry the mercurial vibrations of the plant and the volatile sulphur into the receiver. A dark soup is left behind, pour this into an evaporating dish and gently evaporate off the liquid until you have a sticky oil, in which is locked the fixed sulphur of the plant.

Once this has been achieved, we calcinate both the dead plant and the fixed sulphur and wash these salts in the usual way, making sure we deliquesce the salts under a waxing moon.

c) The plant sulphur after calcination

We now have three products: the clear tincture or 'essence,' containing the plant's Mercury and volatised Sulphur; the plant Salts; and the fixed Salt of Sulphur. Place the clear tincture in a clean retort and pour on the warm salts, hermetically seal and then distil gently. You will notice the clear tincture change colour into golden yellow or sometimes reddish amber. After the first distillation, recohobat the spirit over the salts and repeat the operation until you notice the salts become almost waxy looking, this might take four or five further distillations and recohobations. Once complete, remove the salts, grind, calcinate and wash before placing them in a pelican (circulatory vessel) and pour over

a) Having calcined both the dead plant and the fixed sulphur we extract the water soluble salts using distilled rain water.

the tincture. Seal the pelican and then place in the incubator or cupboard to circulate for a philosophical month (40 days) and then bottle and store for use. The difference between this and the previous recipe is that an elixir is an al-chemically prepared product, made so by the constant distillation and recoho-bations over the plant salts, which volatises them so they can be carried over the receiver with the tincture. When the elixir is complete, circulate in a pelican or other suitable vessel and as the tincture circulates you will notice a 'frost' form inside the glass, a sure sign the salts of the plant have been volatised. We now have a highly actuated product, refined and prepared according to our art and one that will initiate us into the plant's genus, stimulating and awakening our physical, as well as psychic centres. Elixirs are to be taken in water or wine or in-deed directly onto your tongue, only a few drops are necessary a few times a day.

b) The sal salis and the fixed salt of sulphur, first extraction.

ELIXIR SUBTILITATIS

'Fifthly,' says our guide, describing the virtues of five elixirs, 'another shall be appended which is truly noble by the force of its great subtlety: for it resists all the enemies of Nature, by which resistance it never suffers the body to fall into disease.'

Take oil of olive, honey, rectified spirit of wine, of each a pint. Distill them all together in ashes. Then separate all the phlegm from the oils which will be distinguished by many colors. Put all these colors into a pelican, and add to them the third part of the essence of balm and sallendine, and digest them for the space of a month. Then keep it for use. The liquor is so subtle that it penetrates everything.

THE GREAT ESSENCE (ESSENTIA MAGNA)

Rosemary, Lavender, Sage, Marjoram, Thyme, Balm, Angelica, all full of juice, bruise all in a mortar diligently, pour on a sufficient quantity of malmsey-wine (some say of their own spirit or tincture), then in a vessel with a blind head set it to digest in balneo with a gentle heat for two months, express all with a press, calcine the fæces and extract a crystalline or sweet salt which add anon. This expressed juice or wine digest for two months, as before, till a glorious liquor be separated from the fæces or sediment which decant,

The author of this recipe goes on to say:

Its virtues are so great that they can scarcely be numbered; for it strengthens all the inward parts, perfectly cures consumptions, all diseases of the head, heart, breast and lungs, and makes a sad, drooping spirit merry; it cures plague, malign fevers, small-pox, poisons, etc. It is in vain to enumerate its virtues (as curing the vertigo, epilepsy, megrim, convulsions, palsy, etc.), but rather advising all to have it by them upon any occasion.

Take a few drops morning, noon and night in soup, white wine or warm milk.

THE MYSTERY OF THE ELIXIR PROPRIETATIS

Our final inquiry into the confection of elixirs would be amiss without the Elixir Proprietatis. It was said by the author to be of great service, especially to those suffering old age. In the *Book of Formulas* we read: 'It is one of the greatest vegetable cordials, and perfectly cureth consumptions, comforting nature, reviving the heart, and cheering all the spirits, natural, vital and animal.' According to another account: '...the Elixir proprietatis of Paracelsus cureth the Asthmah, the falling sickness (epilepsy), Appoplexy, Palsey, Atrophia, Tabes or the consumption of the lungs.'

It is a rarely attempted work, but one which we believe has incredible virtues and, more importantly, will encourage us to think like an alchemist, which we believe is the greatest lesson. Firstly, let us consider Paracelsus's recipe.

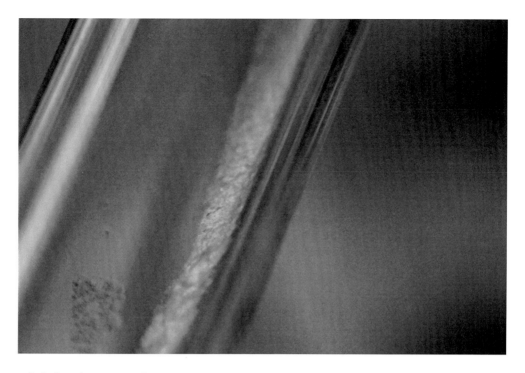

Volatile plant salts coming over the receiver

THE SIXTH ELIXIR, WHICH IS THAT OF PROPRIETY

Equally from natural objects a perfect elixir can be extracted, as out of myrrh, saffron, and alöepatic. As to what forces it proceeds from, that we set down in our treatise on the Generations thereof. Here we only put forth the process, leaving the origin, which we often treat of elsewhere.

Take of myrrh, of alöepaticus, and of saffron, each a quarter of a pound. Put these all together into a pelican, set them in sand, and let them ascend for a month. Then separate the oil from the dregs by means of an alembic without burning. This oil suffer to digest for a month, together with circulatum of equal weight. Afterwards preserve it. In this elixir are all the virtues of the natural balsam, and, moreover, such a conservative virtue for old persons, more than it seems right to assign to it. For not only one period of life seems to proceed from it, but four, seven or ten. It is scarcely possible to express its force and natural powers, but, so far as our judgement goes it has been sufficiently elucidated, nor do we think it requires fuller explanation.

Another account of this mystery,[1] from a short tract by J.H., includes a rendition of Paracelsus's recipe, whilst including the recipes of Van Helmont and the great Crollius. The second recipe belongs to Van Helmont:

> Take Best Myrrh, bright Alloes, of the best saffron, of each one ounce, if thou take more thou shalt find it done in vain; let the first two be beaten, and the saffron role it into a round Figure, put them into a large Glass with a long neck, and seal it hermetically, and digest them in a gently heat, for fear of breaking the Glass, until you see the whole lump grow to the bottom of the glass, and a clear Oyl and Water circulate in the sides of the glass, then open the glass, and pour in a pint of cinnamon water, and distil it in moist sand until no more will ascend: with this medicine, saith he, I have as well dissolved Quartan Agues as continual Feavers, so that he who over night had taken the Holy Sacrament, and received his Sacro Sanctum Viaticum, and the extreme unction of oyl, hath had me his guest by his Bed at dinner.

As mentioned the author then gives Paracelsus's recipe, which is markedly different, but is curious in that after allowing the ingredients to digest for two months, the matter is separated in an alembic with a gentle heat, the *oyl* is then digested for a further month before use. There is no mention of the circulatum in this edition and the author moves on to cite Crollius's recipe:

> Take Myrrh, Alloes, Saffron, of each four Ounces, powder them, and pour on them so much Alcalizate Spirit of Wine, as will reduce them into the form of paste, then pour in so much Oyl of Sulphur made by a Bell Hill as will colour them black, then pour on Spirit of Wine tartarised as will cover

---

1 'A Treatise of The Great Antidote of Van Helmont, Paracelsus and Crollius; By them Called the Elixir Proprietatis: Known by all Physicians to be the greatest Cordial and onely Medicine in the World For long and sound Life, restoring Nature even at the point of Death, and effectually taking away the Seeds of all DISEASES.' Written by J.H., a Lover of Truth and made public for the good of all people, 1668.

them 4 Fingers over, put them in a glass in digestion for two days, separate the tincture, and pour on pure Spirit of Wine, circulate it two months, separate the tincture and distil the fecis by a gentle heat.

Finally our elusive author reveals his own recipe, which might shed some light on this mystery:

Take the best Myrrh, bright Alloes, of the best English Saffron, put them into a Bolt-head, and pour on them a pint and a half of volatile salt of Tartar, volatised with Spirit of Wine, digest them in a gentle heat, till the gummousness be fully gone, and there remain no more bitterness then is contained in the saffron; then separate the pure spirit from the fecis and keep it for use. This Elixir thus prepared, will in colour resemble the pure Arterial Blood of a sound and healthy man; and in taste will be fragrant, in which the Myrrh and Saffron will plainly appear very strong in taste, without any offensiveness or nauseousness, but grateful to the stomach.

However, he is circumspect on the matter of the volatised Tartar Salt:

Now, that I may not tantalise the reader, in mentioning the virtues of the volatile salt of Tartar, and not shewing the way to make it, therefore I shall express it as far as it is lawful. Take of red Tartar, calcine it till be white, then dissolve it in Spirit of Wine, twice its weight such as will burn having Gunpowder in it, till it fire the powder, and continue feeding it three months, until the Salt and Spirit sublime together.

There follow a number of quotes from Van Helmont's *Treatise of Feavers*,[2] at the end of which he states:

It is sufficient for me that Salt of Tartar volatised, and reduced in the Shop of the Stomach, unto the form of meats, passeth into the Meseraick veins; or being conveyed thither by the Urine, doth cleanse all obnoxious humours there congealed. If foulness shall adhere to the first Vessels (the body), we

2 Van Helmont, A *Treatise of the Great Antidote of Van Helmont, Paracelsus and Crollius; by them called the Elixir Proprietatis*, London 1668.

a) First pour the clear distillate into a retort.

b) Next add the both salts and hermetically seal. Vaseline is an excellent means of sealing the joints.

may use cleansing Medicines, Nature safely doing the rest; But if stubborn obstructions shall secretly lodge in a more inward part, the Volatile Alcalies are to be made use of, which wash away the causes of disease as soap washes linen.

We are faced with a number of problems. Firstly, there are disparities between the ingredients (and differing quantities); Paracelsus calls the third alöepaticus, other writers refer to it as Alloes or Bright Alloes. Our search has led us to two possible contenders, firstly Lignum Aloes, often referred to and used by the ancients and in our common tongue called Agarwood. Secondly, the Aloe plant, of which there are at least 350 species, the most famous being Aloe Vera. Both have healing properties.

c) Note the change in the tincture. Once the point of dryness has almost been reached, gather the salts, calcine and return the clear distillate over them again and repeat a further seven times.

The clue is in the term *aloepatic* or *aloe hepatic* which was used to describe the plant's clarity and purity (the terms socotrine, which refers to the island where it grows in abundance and caballine have also been used), rather than a particular genus of the species. Both Thunberg and Antoine de Jussieu would confirm this, with Jussieu witnessing all three varieties being made from the Aloe vulgaris, often called Clear Aloes or Aloe lucida, which would offer us a reason as to why the ancient masters called them Bright Aloes.

The second problem we face is the use of Paracelsus's *circulatum*; Van Helmont uses cinnamon water, Crollius uses Oil of Sulphur, whereas our author reveals that none other than the salt of Tartar volatised by the spirit of wine is suitable. Herein lies the mystery. The definition of the term *circulatum* is hidden behind a number of meanings; it could mean the Grand Elixir, another term for the Philosopher's Stone, making it a highly unlikely contender; the Lesser Cir-

Once complete, place in a suitable circulation vessel and place in an incubator. The circulation of the final product is essential in exalting the elixir. The plant salts frosting the glass have been carried by the spirit – it is a sign that we have successfully volatized the plant salts.

culatum of Urbigerus,[1] which is akin to the vegetable stone and has the ability to reduce all plants and vegetables into their three essentials; a vegetable Alkahest; the volatisation or circulation of the plant salts; or a Work carried out upon Sea Salt.

Since our author, by his own admittance refrains from speaking, we cannot trust his recipe to the letter and therefore we must make our own enquiry and we must separate the wheat from the chaff.

1 In aphorism XXII of his *Circulatum Minus*, Urbigerus writes: *If myrrh, aloes or saffron, each in equal quantity, is put into this Menstruum, then the true Elixir Proprietatis (as Paracelsus calls it), which is an excellent cordial and as efficient and virtuous as the Universal Elixir itself by healing all curable disorders, will presently float the top and its Caput Mortem will separate from it and fall to the bottom.*

We strongly doubt it is the Grand Elixir, and we also question whether he means a specific plant Alkahest, lleaving us with Paracelsus's Circulatum and the volatisation of the plant salts.[2]

As we have mentioned, this is a work of sea salt and one that will require a deeper examination as the terms describe different recipes such as 'dissolved salt,' the Lesser Circulatum; the Greater Circulatum, or Spirit of Salt, and the Quintessence of Salt. We will here consider the volatisation of the plant salts, the work on salt will be reserved for *The White Book*.

When Van Helmont refers to the salts as Salt of Tartar he is not referring to common Potassium Carbonate, but the 'Volatile Alcalies,' and he admonishes us when he says: *Quod si autem ad istud ignis arcanum non pertingatis, discite saltem, salem tartari reddere volatilem...*[3]

We close this chapter with our provisional conclusions only, for we aim to unravel this mystery throughout the course of our work. The first key we will try will be the volatisation of the plant salts, which is discussed in the chapter on magisteries, and so we end our inquiry into the Elixir of Propriety.

---

2 We consider Weidenfield's thoughts on the matter in our following work.

3 *If you cannot attain to that hidden fire* (the Alkahest), *at least learn to make the Salt of Tartar Volatile ...*

Hartmann's Primum Ens Melissæ

First Entities

All herbs, flowers, trees, and other things which proceed out of the Earth, are books, and magick signs, communicated to us, by the immense mercy of God, which signs are our medicine.   – CROLLIUS

In the last three lessons we have created alchemically prepared products and, more importantly, explored a number of alchemical techniques and secrets. The following lesson will discuss how to extract the Primum Ens, or the first entity, from both herbs and human blood. This work was first elucidated in Paracelsus's *The Book Concerning Renovation and Restoration* and is probably the most famous and most practiced of all the recipes he has left us. Unfortunately, many modern alchemists prepare the Ens incorrectly and therefore miss what is most precious.

The Primum Ens, whether it be released from a stone, a pearl, a metal, a herb or an animal, is the first beginnings of an entity or thing, and is considered to be its spiritual substance made manifest. It possesses the highest medicinal properties. As we will see, Paracelsus has left us a number of recipes to extract the First Entity of things, but in our enquiry we are only interested in one.

'The First Entity of balm,' says Paracelsus, 'renovates and restores the body far more powerfully than seems possible to be done in natural things.'

We can confect the Primum Ens from any herb, but in his writings Paracelsus cites two in particular, Melissa and Celandine; both are said to renovate and restore man's body to the prime of life. We have a singular account witnessed of the Primum Ens Melissae by Lesebure, a physician to Louis XIV, quoted by Hartmann, who records the following:

One of my most intimate friends prepared the Primum Ens Melissae, and his curiosity would not allow him to rest until he had seen with his own eyes the effect of this arcanum, so that he might be certain whether or not the accounts given of its virtues were true. He therefore made the experiment, first upon himself, then upon an old female servant aged seventy years, and afterwards upon an old hen that was kept at his house. First he took, every morning at sunrise, a glass of white wine that was tinctured with this remedy, and after using it for fourteen days his finger and toenails began to fall out, without, however causing any pain. He was not courageous enough to continue the experiment, but gave the same remedy to the old female servant. She took it every morning for about ten days, when she began to menstruate again, as in former days. At this she was very much surprised, because she did not know that she had been taking a medicine. She became frightened, and refused to continue the experiment. My friend took, therefore, some grain, soaked in that wine, and gave it to the old hen to eat, and on the sixth day that bird began to lose its feathers, but before two weeks had passed away, new feathers grew, which were much more beautifully coloured; her comb stood up again, and she began again to lay eggs.[1]

We shall examine a number of receipts, the first by Hartmann, a biographer of Paracelsus, who openly admits he knows very little of practical lab alchemy.[2] It is from Hartmann[3] we have received the incorrect recipe; it follows thus:

1 Hartmann, 1896.

2 Hartmann in *Occult Science in Medicine* writes: 'Not being masters of Alchemy, we are not capable of teaching the science of this pillar of medicine; neither could any information in regard to the way in which certain mysterious powers are used be of any service to those who, not having developed these powers, are not in possession of them.' We mention this fact, not to discredit Hartmann's work (since I believe he makes some very worthy observations, uses extensive quotes and references throughout his works and, although Blavatsky found him a bore, I think he is worth reading) but wish only to observe that his experience of practical lab alchemy is limited.

3 Hartmann, 1896. See Appendix 'The Primum Ens.' This is the only recipe I am aware of that includes potassium carbonate as an ingredient in the Primum Ens Melissæ.

HARTMANN'S RECIPE: PRIMUM ENS MELISSÆ

Take half a pound of pure carbonate of potash and expose it to the air until it is dissolved (by attracting water from the atmosphere). Filter the fluid, and put as many fresh leaves of the plant melissa into it as it will hold, so that the fluid will cover the leaves. Let it stand in a well closed glass, and in a moderately warm place, for twenty four hours. The fluid may then be removed from the leaves, and the latter thrown away. On the top of this fluid absolute alcohol is poured, so that it will cover the former to the height of one or two inches, and it is left to remain for one or two days, or until the alcohol becomes of an intensely green colour. This alcohol is then to be taken away and preserved and fresh alcohol is put upon the alkaline fluid, and the operation is repeated until all the colouring matter is absorbed by the alcohol. This alcoholic fluid is now to be distilled, and the alcohol evaporated until it becomes the thickness of a syrup, which is the Primum Ens Melissae; but the alcohol that has been distilled away and the liquid potash may be used again. The liquid potash must be of great concentration and the alcohol of great strength, else they would become mixed, and the experiment would not succeed.

Hartmann's mistake is to translate the 'dissolved salts' as being potassium carbonate, *per deliquium*, providing us with what alchemists call the Oil of Tartar. Paracelsus's own recipe, the True Primum Ens, is markedly different, but first, let us investigate Hartmann's recipe.

To begin we will need to prepare ourselves a suitable 'magnet' capable of drawing from the stars and moon. Herein lies the Astral Fire and therefore we will need a quantity of Potassium Carbonate or Potash or, as the ancients knew it, Salt of Tartar[4] to investigate this recipe. Potassium Carbonate is a necessary ingredient for later alchemical works, especially when purifying the Regulus, so a regular supply of it will be required.

If one has an open fire gather the ashes and keep them aside, otherwise ashes from barbeques or bonfires would be suitable. Ideally they should be from hard woods like oak.

4 When the old alchemists refer to salt of tartar they mostly mean potassium carbonate, but when reading Hollandus it can also mean the salts of the plant being worked.

Potassium Carbonate or Potash,
sometimes called Salt of Tartar by
the Alchemists, is extracted from
wood ash and prepared.

Pour the salts on a glass dish,
(choose a cheap one as they will
score the glass mercilessly), and
place them in a dry spot
under a waxing moon.

The resultant liquid, Oil of Tartar,
once distilled in a retort or alembic,
is referred to as 'Aqua Angelis.'
The salts can be reclaimed, dried
and used again.

Once these ashes have been collected, put them in a bucket or suitable receptacle and pour rainwater over them until they are entirely covered. Stir them and leave the ash to settle. Filter the water and evaporate, at which point you will notice a white salt forming (*coagula*). Solve et coagula, or wash with distilled rainwater calcinating to a pure white in a furnace or fire.

When white as snow, grind. As Hartmann relates, Potassium Carbonate is hydroscopic and will 'suck' the moisture from the air, therefore when they are ready, place on a flat glass dish and allow them to deliquesce under a waxing moon. Make sure you leave them in a shaded place to avoid contamination by rain. Then carefully gather the liquid, which the alchemists call Oil of Tartar, and set aside until at least 250 ml of liquid has been gathered. Even though this is not the true method of the Primum Ens Melissæ, if we distil the oil of Tartar we will have what the ancients called *Aqua Angelis*. To prepare the Aqua Angelis pour the Oil of Tartar into a retort or alembic, hermetically seal, and distill at a gentle heat. The remaining salts can be used again. This makes an excellent menstruum to use across other herbal works as it is charged with the astral fire.

When we have enough Oil of Tartar, gather the herb on a waxing moon in the day and hour of Jupiter, and grind in a mortar. Many modern alchemists use a food blender, though purists frown on this approach saying that the metal 'determines' the plant. In my experience, one can achieve perfect products using both methods; the benefits of working the plant material by hand is that it allows one's consciousness to influence the final product, but it can be a long and drawn out process.

Fresh lemon balm

When finally ground to a pap, place in a suitable flask and pour on Oil of Tartar. The liquid will immediately turn green; shake and leave in a warm place for 24 hours. Remove the dead herb and add fresh plant material. Again, this is best when cut in the planetary hour of the plant.

Once the liquid is saturated remove the dead plant from the menstruum and pour on highly rectified spirit of wine. Be warned, the spirit of wine needs to be extremely strong. If you have succeeded in this, the spirit of wine will rest on top of the oil of tartar. Set aside for twenty four hours. Notice how the clear layer of alcohol draws into itself the First Entity of the Melissa, tincturing it

We must use highly rectified spirit of wine or this work shall be in vain.

into either a beautiful bottle green or a golden yellow. The Oil of Tartar will also change colour, turning a deep ruby red, with the potassium carbonate settling at the bottom, which can be washed, calcinated and used again. Separate the Ens by placing into a separating funnel or by simply using a pipette and allow the alcohol to evaporate naturally in a warm room until a honey-like oil is left. As we shall see, this is not the true Ens, for the true Ens, in Paracelsus's own words, will fulfil the following conditions:

> Let either of those first entities be put into good wine, in such quantity that it may be tinged therewith. Having done this, it is prepared for this regimen. Some of this wine must be drunk every day about dawn until first of all the nails fall off from the fingers, afterwards from the feet, then the hair and teeth and, lastly, the skin be dried up and a new skin be produced.
>
> When all this is done that medicament or potion must be discontinued. And again, new nails, hair and fresh teeth are produced, as well as the new skin and all diseases of the body and mind pass away, as was declared above.

We have made Hartmann's recipe a number of times and, although I felt an increase in energy, creativity and general vitality, at no point did my hair, teeth and nails fall out!

Let us now consider the original recipe written by Paracelsus's own hand. The mystery is hidden in the terms *digestion* and, more importantly, *dissolved salts*, which he uses in the extraction of the First Entity of Herbs, Gems and Sulphur. By unlocking this secret we unlock the rest of Paracelsus's First Entities and more importantly, the true Primum Ens Melissae; take note, gentle philosopher.

THE FIRST ENTITY OF HERBS

Take celandine or balm; beat them into a pulse, shut them up in a glass vessel hermetically sealed, and place in horse dung to be digested for a month. Afterwards separate the pure from the impure, pour the pure into a glass vessel with dissolved salt, and let this, when closed, be exposed to the sun for a month. When this period has elapsed, you will find at the bottom a thick liquid and the salt floating on the surface. When this is separated you will have the virtues of the balm or of the celandine, as they are in their first entity; and these are called, and really are, the first entities of the balm or of the celandine.

If we do not look closely at the procedure it becomes barely workable, for as well as the digestion process the term *dissolved salt*[1] is ambiguous. We must examine other recipes if we are to unravel this mystery.

The following receipt for the Primum Ens has been drawn from the *Book of Formulas*, which uses alchemical symbolism to describe the work and does much to clarify the process. We have translated those symbols, but otherwise leave the recipe intact:

In the proper season of the year, when the herb (balm) is at its full growth, and, consequently, its juices in their whole vigour, gather at the fittest time

---

1 As we have mentioned there are far too many secrets in the Work on Salt to numerate in this volume. For now the term *Dissolved salts* (alternatively *lesser circulatum*) and *Circulated Salts* can be understood as being Water of Salt or Spirit of Salt respectively.

of the day, (when Jupiter is rising and the Moon in Cancer is applying to a conjunction, sextile, or trine aspect thereto), a sufficient quantity of balm, wipe it clean, and pick it; then put it in a stone mortar, and by laborious beating reduce it into a thin pap. Take this glutinous and odoriferous substance and put it into a bolthead, which is to be hermetically sealed, place it in a dunghill, or some gentle heat equivalent thereto where it must be digested for forty days. When it is taken out the matter will appear clearer than ever, and have a quicker scent. Then separate the grosser parts, which, however, are not to be thrown away. Put this liquid into a gentle bath, that the remaining gross particles may perfectly subside. In the meantime dry, calcinate, and extract the fixed salt of the grosser parts (which remained after the above separation), which fixed salt is to be joined to the liquor when filtrated. Next take sea salt, well purified, melt it, and, by setting it in a cold place (deliquesce), it will dissolve and become clear and limpid. Take of both liquors *ana*, mix them thoroughly, and having hermetically sealed them in a proper glass, let them be carefully exposed to the sun, in the warmest season of the year, for about six weeks. At the end of this space the *primum ens* of the balm will appear swimming on the top like a bright green oil, which is to be carefully separated and preserved.

Of this oil, a few drops taken in a glass of wine for several days together, will bring to pass those wonders that are reported of the Countess of Desmond[1] and others; for it will entirely change the juices of the human body, reviving the decaying frame of life, and restoring the spirits of long-lost youth.

To test the efficacy of this mystery, the author suggests the following:

1 It appears the Countess of Desmond was quite a celebrity in that she lived for 140 years of age in perfect health having re-grown three sets of teeth throughout the course of her life. The following is taken from the *Dublin Review*: The Earl of Leicester's reminiscences were personally communicated to Sir William Temple, and are retailed in his essay 'Of Heath and Long Life,' published in his *Miscellanies 1689*, in the following terms: 'The late Robert Earl of Leicester, who was a person of great learning and observation, as well as of truth, told me several stories very extraordinary on this subject; one, of a Countess of Desmond, married out of England in Edward IV's time, and who lived far in King James' reign, and was counted to have died some years above a hundred and forty: at which age she came from Bristol to London to beg some relief at Court, having long been very poor by the ruin of that Irish family into which she was married.' We are told she died from a fever caused by falling from a tree, which she was climbing to gather nuts.

The mystery of 'dissolved salt.' It is a work we shall further examine in The White Book.

If after the medicine is thus prepared any doubt be had of its efficacy, or
of its manner of operation, let a few drops be given every day on raw meat
to any old dog or cat, and in less than a fortnight, by the changing of their
coats and other incontestable changes, the virtue of this preparation will
sufficiently appear.

The use of sea salt in this recipe is explicit and the process of deliquescing sea
salt would appear to confirm our suspicions that potash is not the salt Paracelsus
is referring to in his preparation of the Ens Melissae; we do, however, have another contender and that is Johann Rudolph Glauber's 'fiery liquor.' It is a work
which we will explore and one we believe will help us answer the Mystery of
First Entities, but for now our concluding recipe comes from John French's *Art
of Distillation*, though not named the Primum Ens, it has a striking similarity to
Paracelsus's own recipe. Of worthy note is the digestion process and the use of
what French calls the Spirit of Salt. He names this recipe:

THE QUINTESSENCE OF ALL VEGETABLES

Take of what spices, flowers, seeds, herbs, woods you please and put them into rectified spirit of wine. Let the spirit extract in digestion until no more feces fall to the bottom but all their essence is gone into the spirit of wine. Upon being thus impregnated, pour a strong spirit of salt and digest it in Balneum until an oil swims above which separate with a tunnel or draw of the spirit of wine in balneum. The oil will remain clear at the bottom, but before the spirit of wine is abstracted, the oil is blood red and a true quintessence.[1]

1 Glauber's recipe, after French: 'Pour upon Spices, Seeds, Woods, Roots, Fruits, Flowers, & c. the Spirit of Wine well rectified, place them in digestion to be extracted, until all the essence be extracted, with the Spirit of Wine; then upon this Spirit of Wine, being impregnated, pour the best Spirit of Salt; and being thus mixed together, place them in Balneo to digest, until the Oil be separated, and swim above from the Spirit of Wine, then separate it with a separating glass, or distil off the Spirit of Wine in Balneo, and a clear Oil will ascend; for if the Spirit of Wine be not abstracted, then that Oil will be as red as blood; and it is the true quintessence of that vegetable,

Paracelsus suggests digesting the herb for 40 days until it is clear. Using the herb alone proved fruitless in obtaining this liquid and therefore we believe he accidently breezed over the digestion process, left it occult or did not mention it because the process would have been common knowledge. If we examine his work as a whole, we later find in his *Archidoxies*, Paracelsus making the following addition: '...by dissolving water is to be understood the water of salt.'[1] And a few paragraphs later he confirms:

> But since frequent mention is made in our Archidoxies of First Entities, and since the chief foundation is hidden in them, we will here briefly add the preparation of our water of circulated salt, which is here required, but was omitted.

French's recipe also sheds light on the digestion process, of which Paracelsus makes little mention. To this point the following advice, concerning digestion, is well worth observing; from *The Book of Formulas*:

> In most instances of digestion and putrefaction, and more especially where a quintessence is the end to be attained, a homogene menstruum – as the spirits, phlegm, or water of the subject matter itself – is absolutely a requisite, that the astral principles inherent therein be not fatally disturbed, or their efficacy impaired. As saith Paracelsus, 'Every fruit must die in that wherein is its life.'

With these words we temporarily conclude our investigation into the Primum Ens and, like Paracelsus before us, we omit a more detailed investigation for we shall explore, in greater detail, his Circulated Salts in *The White Book*.

from whence by the Spirit of Wine it was extracted.' From *The Works of the Highly Experienced and Famous Chymist John Rudolph Glauber*. Thomas Milbourn, London 1689.

1 *The Tenth Book of the Archidoxies*, chapter III, 'Concerning Magisteries.'

Magisteries

As we penetrate further into the tangled briars of the philosophers' garden we are in danger of becoming snared in language and terms which are often contradictory. Some are blinds, some are riddles, some poetical flair, whilst others are just plain and simple ignorance. We must also remember these old artists worked alone and would have perfected their own recipes and processes which when brought together, as we have endeavoured to do in this work, become mixed and contradictory. The term *magistery* is no exception.

The Philosophers of Nature, a group of practicing alchemists under the tutelage of Jean Dubuis, aim to provide a single process, whilst Paracelsus offers numerous examples, Hollandus still more. All are worthy of consideration, not just for their virtue, but also their modus operandi. This is an occult alchemical process, hidden even by modern masters, and it will teach us much, especially how to approach the Kingdom of Metals.

As mentioned in Hollandus's *Opera Vegetabile*, which we will discuss in more detail, the alkali salts are not entirely digested in the stomach and nor is the plant sulphur, the rest being expelled by the body. In our work on elixirs we have seen how the salts are volatised by constant recohobation of the tincture over the body – a plant magistery as performed by the students of the Philosophers of Nature volatises the salts over the essential oil.

A plant magistery elevates a herb, making it more penetrating and has similar properties to a plant stone. Indeed, a plant magistery has been called a 'liquid stone' in that when we confect it we will require more Sulphur than Salt and Mercury. The old masters have deliberately withheld the volitisation or subli-

Plant salts volatizing

mation of the plant salts (and for that matter the animal and mineral) from their works, for it is the key by which we open the last door. Even today, initiates speaking of the plant kingdom do not share this secret wilfully; and yet if we are to proceed we must master this mystery. It is one of the highest alchemical preparations one can create and one that will have a profound and invigorating effect on the system, if, that is, it is birthed according to our Art. Firstly, we shall examine Paracelsus's recipe:

> Herbs, however, and other things of that kind, must be mixed with *vinum ardens*,[1] and putrefied with it for a month. Then they must be distilled by the *balneum maris*,[2] and that which is distilled must be again poured on. This must be repeated until the whole quantity of *vinum ardens* shall be four times less than the juices of the herbs. Distil this in a pelican, with new additions for a month, and then separate it. When you have done this, you shall have the magistery of that matter or that herb which you selected.

1 Rectified spirit of wine.
2 Water bath, but a heating mantle will suffice.

For this recipe we will use dried herbs, which can either be previously gathered and dried, or bought from an herbal supplier. Although we can make an alchemical magistery from any ally, some are not as rich in volatile sulphur as other herbs and in some cases will require more plant material. Therefore let us choose a herb like caraway, thyme, or rosemary, as all these are rich in essential oils.

We will need a more sophisticated distillation setup than our alembic and retort and therefore we will be using a condenser attached to an aquarium pump. Since some plants' volatised oils separate under different temperatures and since plant life is very delicate and susceptible to high degrees of heat, this distillation set up is important to lower the temperature. To reduce the heat even further a vacuum pump can be used. The ancients would have created a vacuum by immersing the receiving flask in hot water and allowing it to cool, which created an effective means of drawing the oils over at low temperatures.

MAGISTERY OF LAVENDER

Place the herb in a glass flask and cover in distilled rainwater and allow to soak for at least 24 hours. Fasten a condenser to the flask and a separator to the condenser and distil the volatised sulphur, which will come over into the separator and rest on top of the water. Depending on the size of your flask the extraction of the plant sulphur might have to be done in batches, in which case squeeze the dead plant material and add fresh herb to the flask with the plant soup and allow to soak for another 24 hours before commencing the second extraction. Continue the process until the entire herb has been used.[3]

We will have a dark soup remaining as well as the plant body. Squeeze the plant body dry and evaporate the soup, which contains the fixed salt of sulphur.

We now have our volatile sulphur, the plant salts and the fixed salt of sulphur, and we are in a position to take our work down one of two paths, creating either an elixir or a plant stone. Since we're exploring the volatisation of our tartar salts we will prepare for the elixir, which is in fact a volatile plant stone.

RECIPE

Lavender
Distilled Rainwater
Distillation train
Sandbath or
Heating mantle

3 Hint: A thick black ring might appear round the inside of the flask. This is burnt plant sulphur due to too much heat. Lower the temperature and either create more vacuum by warming the receiving flask in warm water before attaching or raise the flask containing the plant matter so it rests a few millimetres from the surface of the heating mantle.

a) Lavender

b) Extract the essential oil

c) Calcinate the Caput Mortum, the dead body

d) Wash the ash with distilled water

e) Evaporate the water

f) Gather the prepared salts

g) Add the salts to the sulphur

Seal the retort and distill

Once we have purified both salts, washing them in distilled rainwater and calcinating them to a whiteness no less than seven times, grind them to a powder.
When ready, we pour our volatile sulphur in a retort and allow to cool. At this
point add the salts a tea spoon at a time. As the salts hit the oil there will be a
fierce reaction and herein lies the missing key. What would make these salts react so fiercely with the sulphur? Meditate on the problem and you will discover
the solution; this secret is not mine to disclose.

Once the salts have been spooned onto the sulphur, seal the retort and gently
distil the oil; we do not want too much heat as this will spatter the helm of the
retort. As we near the end of our first distillation, the first flight of the eagles
as it was known by the ancients, the sulphur in the retort will darken and there
will appear along the neck and sometimes at the upper part at the top of the
retort a frosted clear salt. Return the distillate back over the caput mortuum,
seal the retort and repeat the process making sure you allow the retort to cool
before recohobating the oil over the body. This time you may notice less volatised salt in the neck of the retort; this is because the second flight of the eagles

The plant salts volatizing

has washed the neck of the retort carrying the volatised salts with it. During the third distillation you will notice the salts reappear and on the fourth distillation they will once more be washed into the receiver by the oil. By the sixth and final distillation you will again see a frosting on the glass. Distil the residue almost to the dry and keep aside the distillate. We now have an essential oil saturated with the volatised salts, but much of the plant salts remains in the neck of the retort. To wash these out we carefully add 150ml of rectified spirit of wine and add a clean receiving flask to the retort; distil gently and the mercury will wash the remaining volatised salt into the receiver.

We now have a mercury, carrying the volatised salts and oil which has been repeatedly saturated with plant salts. We combine them in equal measure into a pelican or circulatory vessel and allow them to circulate in a closed heat for a philosophical month. As we have stated previously, this constant circulation will allow the product to 'breathe' and mature, thus elevating its nature. Indeed, the longer we leave our Majesty in circulation, the stronger it will be.

If you have managed t o suc ceed in volatising your plant salts, you have achieved what others have not achieved. You will have created a highly potent alchemical product as well as learning some valuable lessons that will allow you to approach the Great Work.

THE MAGISTERY OF BLOOD

There is, likewise, reckoned a special magistery of the blood, which is taught in a peculiar form and manner. In it is considered what virtues and forces of man exist, and what its nature contains in itself, in what there is any defect produced, and so on; but still, without diminution of the natural creation, but that it may be considered as a complete and perfect work in all its parts, as a bird with all its feathers.[1]

A friend once told me a story about an associate of his who had a terminally ill child. Being spiritually inclined they sought help from various sources with no result until they happened on an alchemist who prescribed a medicine made from the boy's blood. Suffice to say the boy was cured. It is a rarely practiced work and one worthy of exploration.

1 Paracelsus, *The Sixth Book of the Archidoxies.*

Blood having been incubated for 40 days

Take of the purest blood as much as you please. Put it into a pelican, so that three parts of four may be empty, and then digest it a month in horse dung (in which time it will swell and become as much more as it was when it was put in). Then distill off the phlegm in balneum, and in the bottom will remain the magistery of blood which must be distilled and cohobated nine times in a retort in ashes, and then it is perfected.

This magistery is of excellent virtue which, being taken inwardly, and applied outwardly cures most diseases and eases pain, being very balsamical.[1]

'There are many wonderful virtues, exceeding belief,' in the blood, continues Paracelsus, 'and it is a costly treasure of the whole nature.' It is a work we shall explore in more detail and so we close with Paracelsus's magistery of blood:

Take blood, shut it up in a pelican, and suffer it to rise up so long in a *venter equinus* until the third part of the pelican shall be filled. For all blood in its rectification is dilated according to the quantity, and not according to the weight. When this time is fulfilled you must rectify it by a bath. In this way the phlegms recede, and the magistery remains at the bottom. Having shut this up in a retort, and hermetically sealed it, distil it nine times, as we have taught in the book, *Concerning Preparations*. In this way you will arrive at the magistery of blood.[2]

So we close our examination into the mystery of magisteries.

1 John French, *The Art of Distillation*.
2 Waite points out that the treatise to which Paracelsus refers does not include any reference to the magistery of blood.

The Quintessence

This, then, is worthy to be called an art, which teaches the mysteries of Nature; which by means of the quintessence, can cure a contraction and bring about health in the space of four days, whereas otherwise death would be the result.
        – PARACELSUS

'The quintessence,' writes Paracelsus, 'is a certain matter extracted from all things which Nature has produced, and from everything which has life corporeally in itself, a matter most subtly purged of all impurities and mortality, and separated from all the elements. From this it is evident that the quintessence is, so to say, a nature, a force, a virtue, and a medicine, once, indeed, shut up within things, but now free from any domicile and from all outward incorporation.'

The quintessence represents the purest virtue of a plant, mineral or metal (in terms of quality not quantity) and therefore is the most acute degree of purity in that it is the spirit of life locked within a substance. Interestingly, Paracelsus says that a quintessence cannot be extracted from the flesh of man or animals, in that the spirit of life would not be present, as life exists in the soul.

To suggest a single process by which we can extract the quintessence would be erroneous, since there are many different definitions of this expression and many artists perfected their own way. Eugenius Philalethes states that there is no fifth essence except God, and Waite confirms:

> Wheresoever God is there this train of fire attends him. It was this fire which was manifested to Moses on Mount Sinai. According to another authority, the terms quintessence, specific, magnetism, bond, seed of the pure elements, &c. are all synonyms of one substance, a subject wherein the form abides. It is a material essence, which encloses an operative and celestial spirit. The Quintessence of the Elements is the Mercury of the Philosophers.

Johann Isaac Hollandus, in his *Medicinal Recipes*, aims to clarify the disparities when he writes:

> Wherefore my son, know this: That all that God hath created good in the upper part of the world, are perfect and incorruptible as the heaven. What-soever is in the lower parts, whether it be in beasts, fishes, and all manner of sensible creatures, herbs or plants, it is indued with a double nature. That is to say, both perfect and imperfect. The perfect nature is known as the Quintessence and the imperfect is known as the faeces or dregs, or the venomous or combustible oil. Therefore, you shall separate the dregs and the combustible oil and then, that which remains is perfect and is called the Quintessence, which will endure continually, even as the heavens endure and it can neither be dissolved with fire or any other thing.

He writes extensively on the subject and we shall examine his work in more detail. Firstly however, let us consider Paracelsus's thoughts on the matter:

> Abstract the volatile portion, which passes over in the separation of the elements, several times from that which is fixed, so that the quintessence, which partly was raised with the phlegm, may be again conjoined. Take the fixed element that remained after the separation of the three imperfect elements, of whatsoever sort it may be, then dissolve it in its proper water, each according to its nature, as we have said in the *Archidoxies* concerning the Quintessence. Keep it in the highest state of putrefaction, distil it by cohobation, and the rest by descent. Putrefy still a little, distil, and join all. Then distil it in a Balneum Mariæ, even to oiliness. Then break it up with the subtle spirit of wine by boiling; the impure will sink to the bottom and the pure will float on the surface. Separate this by means of a tritorium, and, in order that it may at the same time lose the nature of the *aqua fortis*, pour on a greater quantity of spirit of wine, which frequently abstract until the quintessence turns out sweet. Lastly, wash it in common cold water. In the same way, it must be understood of marchasites, stones, resins, herbs, flesh, watery and fixed substances...

As we pursue our work in the different kingdoms we will return to the quintessence, but for now I will give a simpler method of extracting the quintessence. Gathered from Paracelsus's writings is the extraction of the quintessence from Spices:[1]

CONCERNING THE EXTRACTION
OF THE QUINTESSENCE FROM SPICES

We will now teach the method of extracting the quintessence from spices, as musk, civet, camphor, and the like.[2] First the quintessence ought to be reduced to another form, and at length to be separated therefrom. In that same process of separation the quintessence is found, in the following way:

Take oil of almonds, with which let an aromatic body be mixed, and let them be digested together in a glass vessel in the sun, for the proper time, until they are reduced to a paste. Afterwards let them be pressed out from their dregs. In this way the body is separated from the quintessence, which is thus mixed with oil, from which it is separated as follows: Take rectified ardent wine, into which let the aforesaid oil be poured, and let them be left in process of digestion for six days. Afterwards let them be distilled by ashes.[3] The ardent wine will ascend, and the quintessence with it. The oil will remain at the bottom without any of the quintessence remaining. Afterwards let this wine be distilled by the *balneum maris*, and the quintessence will remain at the bottom in the form of an oil distinct from all similar ones.

1   For further details see *The Fourth Book of Archidoxies*, in A.E. Waite, *Hermetic and Alchemical Writings of Paracelsus*, vol.II, p.34.
2   Perhaps a more suitable list of spices might be: aniseed, asafoetida, fennel seeds, cumin, black pepper, coriander, caraway, cinnamon, ginger; some authors would even include mint and basil.
3   The *ashes* means what the retort should rest in during the distillation and is used as an alchemist's guide to describe the level of heat necessary.

The True Essence or Rather Quintessence of Any Herb is Made Thus:[1]

When you have made the water and oil of any vegetable first calcine or burn to ashes the remainder of the herb. With the ashes make a lye by pouring its own water thereon. When you have drawn out all the strength of the ashes, then take all the lye, being first filtered, and vapor it away and at the bottom you shall find a black salt which you must take and put into a crucible and melt it in a strong fire (covering the crucible all the time it is melting). After it is melted let it boil half an hour or more. Then take it out and beat it small and set it in a cellar on a marble stone or in a broad glass and it will all be resolved into a liquor. This liquor filter and vapor away the humidity until it be very dry and as white as snow. Then let this salt imbibe as much of the oil of the same vegetable as it can, but no more, lest you labor in vain. Then digest them together until the oil will not rise from the salt, but both become a fixed powder melting with an easy heat.

THE QUINTESSENCE OF HONEY

The power of honey is mentioned and used by the greatest of physicians. Apart from its use as an antiseptic, Paracelsus says one can extract a highly rectified acetum from honey. But for the healing arts Hollandus[2] reveals how to extract its quintessence:

> If God hath given unto other things the gift of healing, what then is there not in Honie, which is gathered from many floures and many herbs, and are all endued with a particular virtue? Truly if it be brought to his height and excellency, it will work marvelously. Now consider what lies hidden in this Quintessence and esteem it not lightly, but keep it secret as the most excellent thing of all Animal work. If this is obtained, you will need no other medicines to put away all accidents of the body.
>
> Now I will set in hand with the practice. Take twelve quarts of the best Virgin Honie and put it in a great earthern vessel with a Limbeck well luted.

1 John French, *The Art of Distillation.*
2 Hollandus, *Medicinal Recipes.*

Set this in Balneo and lute a recipient to the neck of it and distill that which will distill of it, which is boiling in your Balneo. My son, know this, that there is no common water in Honie, but only Philosophical and Elemental. For the element of Aire does pass first together with the element of Fire in which the Aire is contained. The air, when it rises, resembles the savor of Aqua Vitæ distilled. Initially, it can not be distinguished from Aqua Vitæ either by sight or by savor. Distill it then, until no more arises, then leave the vessel in Balneo five days with a Limbeck and receiver. Let it boil night and day that the matter may be dried. Cool it now, take it out and remove the receiver and Limbeck. That which is in the receiver pour back into the vessel over the dry matter. Set it back in Balneo and cover the mouth of the vessel with a clean, well luted dish, and let your Balneum be only lukewarm.

My son, understand that it may thus be done, for it is good that the fire be drawn with his proper air, so as a man would stay so long, for it would be of greater force. The ancient Philosophers wrought in this sort, but the danger is, when the vessels shall be opened, the water may fly away, it being as subtle as wine. For every time the air is to be drawn away, and again to be poured on, making putrefaction in a warm Balneo, but first it must be well luted and a Limbeck being set on with a receiver, you must reiterate the work, until the fire rises like red blood. There is yet another method or rule of working found out in these our days, which is in this sort.

They are thus drawn out and the matter is dried, as has been said. Then take common water which has been twice distilled in Balneo and pour on as much as is sufficient and set in Balneo. Cover the mouth of the vessel but don't let the Balneo boil. Let it stand thus for three days and three nights, moving it day and night with a wooden spatula or spoon that is clean. After this, let it cool, remove it, pour it out and strain it. Then, take a clean vessel and decant the clear liquid and then pour on the Fæces fresh distilled water (rain water is best) as was done before and set the vessel in Balneo as before. Let it be cleared and put aside with the first water and pour once more fresh distilled (rain) water and once again set in Balneo. Do this as often as the water is tincted or coloured. When it no longer is tinged, you have separated the fire from the earth. Reserve the earth, or Fæces, until I tell you further what to do with it, for there is a combustible oil in it.

Take the vessel containing the colored water and set it in Balneo with a

Limbeck and receiver well luted. Diſtill all the water with a boiling Balneo and let the matter be well dried and cool. Then take away the Limbeck and let the vessel remain in Balneo and pour on again (from the receiver) the water over the matter and make a fire. Set a dish upon the mouth of the vessel and let it ſtand in Balneo three days. Stir this every day, three or four times with a clean wooden spatula. After this, let it cool, remove it and filter it. Then take a clean vessel and carefully decant the clear liquid into the vessel and right away pour on the Fæces fresh diſtilled (rain) water, ſtirring it with a wooden ladle and let it ſtand one day to clear (settle) and the Fæces that remain, put them in with the firſt Fæces which has been set aside. Then take a clean vessel and set it in a boiling Balneo until it is thoroughly dry and repeat this process until there remain no Fæces in the bottom of the vessel. In this way, you shall obtain the pure element of Fire: and the element of Aire muſt also be so often diſtilled until there remains nothing in the bottom. This is the manner in which the pure elements are obtained. Separate then the water from the fire, and let it dry. This will give you a clear shining matter similar to Camphor. Keep the Fire well in a glass contained and the Aire with the Water in another container of glass, well sealed, until you have your earth prepared.

Take all the earth with the faeces and draw out the combuſtible oyle by a discensorie,[1] that is, with two vessels joined together and luted (probably needs a vacuum) until the Combuſtible oil passes. This oil is useful for all cold diseases and other passions. If you do not want the combuſtible oil, juſt let it fly away. Then take your earth and calcine it in a reverbatory furnace, gently, until it be all white as snow. Then take a great earthen or ſtone vessel and put into it this white calcined earth, on which pour a goodly amount of common diſtilled water. Stir it with a wooden ladle and let it ſtand three days in a boiling bath and keep it covered with a dish. Daily, ſtir it a dozen times. Let it cool, remove the vessel and let it ſtand to clear, for one day. Now, take another clean vessel and softly pour out that which is clear (decant). Upon the Fæces, again pour fresh diſtilled water and once again set it in Balneo. Cool, remove, let ſtand one day and decant into the firſt waters thus obtained. A third time pour fresh diſtilled water over the

1 *Descension:* the term is used much by Paracelsus to describe distillation and the definition should be noted by true students of the art.

Fæces and repeat the entire process. The Fæces can now be thrown away as they no longer contain any value.

Take the vessel with these three waters and set it in Balneo with a Limbeck and receiver. With a boiling Balneo, draw out the water until the matter be dry. Let it cool. Take away the Limbeck and pour the water (from the receiver) on the earth again and set it in boiling Balneo for one day. Let it dissolve and clear. Decant that which is clear and put in a little distilled water on the Fæces, and let it stand for two or three hours in a warm bath. Remove it from the bath and allow it to stand for two or three hours and pour out the upper part upon the first waters and the Fæces can be thrown away. Once again set the vessel in Balneo, with the earth, or salt, and distill away the water until all be dry as before. Repeat this work until no Faeces remain in the bottom. Drain away the water from the earth and it will be like Crystal. Pure.

Take a great glass that will bear the heat and put into it your Fire and your Earth and pour your Aire upon it and set it to distill in a furnace, in a pot with sand or ashes, with a Limbeck well luted, having a hole in the uppermost knottie part that a funnel may be put in when there shall be a need of Infusion. When as the humidity that it hath received be half consumed, then fortify your fire a little, gradually until you see the water start to boil. Keep the fire in this state until the liquid boils out so that only a pint remains. Remove the fire, let the glass cool and take away the receiver and open the hole in the Limbeck and put in a glass funnel. (*Note*: The Limbeck is NOT removed from the vessel). Pour in all the water that distilled over into the receiver. Plug the hole in the Limbeck and set the recipient to the neck again and lute it well. Distill again making the same observations and practices as before. Do this ten times. The tenth distillation being complete, let all pass together as the earth is made volatile. So the Aire, the Water, the Fire and the Earth will ascend together by the Limbeck and be brought into one substance which were in four. Once together in nature and now simple as the incorruptible heaven, yet are they not fixed: but notwithstanding they are so coupled together and so intertwined; that by no means can they be separated. They will continue now together as one body, forever; even as the Christalline and uncorruptible heaven, which notwithstanding, is compounded of the four Elements. What do you think of this, my Son? Cannot this Quintessence help every disease that now infects man through his most excellent temperature, whether it be in heat, cold, moist or dry. For all are in it that he may distribute unto every one that which is necessary; even as the heaven when need requireth, gives unto the earth all things as coldness, heat or moisture. And yet, it is neither hot, cold, moist or dry, but of one simple essence, and that imbued with such a nature that it giveth unto everything that which is necessary. In like manner, this is what this Quintessence does. Therefore my son, Rejoice! Give the Almighty God thanks which has opened these things unto the Philosophers.

Now my son, if you would bring this Quintessence to even greater perfection, take a great circulatory or Pelican, that is a great glass that hath a great head similar to a Limbeck, and in the top of the head, a hole by which the matter may be poured in by means of a funnel. This hole is to be stoppered. Out of the head comes two arms bending around into the belly. This permits that which goes up to descend again, through the arms back into the belly of the Pelican. This is the form of the vessel or Pelican, that distills one into the other.

1. Take then your Quintessence and put it into a Pelican and set this into ashes. Better yet, put it into salt, prepared and dried (like a sand bath). Regulate the fire so that it is like the heat in summer, the extreme heat. The Quintessence will rise like red oil and fall down again by the arms of the Pelican. By repeated ascensions, the Quintessence will become thick like wax or syrup. So much so that it will remain in the bottom eventually, and no longer ascend. At this point, fortify your fire so that the Quintessence will again ascend and descend. Maintain this heat until it again will not ascend but remains in the bottom. Make the fire even stronger that it will once again ascend and descend. Keep this same heat until it again rise no more.

2. Observe this manner of augmenting the fire until the water be fixed and the glass turns red hot. This will take about twenty-four hours all-together. If at the end of this time, the Quintessence no longer arises, it is indeed fixed and is brought into his highest virtue. Remove it from the glass while still hot or it will become hard as wax when cooled and you will have to break the glass to remove it. For when hot, like wax it will become liquid. But when cool it congeals and pierces every hard thing, as oil does any leather. Its colour is like a Ruby, and through shining like a Christal, it gives

light in the dark, sufficient to read by. What do you think of this, my son? Are there not many strange bodies created by God? Truly he has imbued the Philosophers with no less gifts, for they that can look into the secrets of nature, shall see it to be an incredible operation. For this is gathered by Bees of the subtlest parts of all plants, trees, floures and fruits, and at that time when floures break out and trees bud. It is worthily called the Philosopher's Stone, for it is fixed and liquifiable as Wax and as the mineral Stone transmutes the impure metals, so does this one alter diseases.

Hereby it appears that this bears the bell among all the Vegetals; whereas it being yet in his grossness and impure, it is but of small value for any use in Physick by whatever means it may be boiled or skimmed off, but always retains his nature because it consists of all the fruits of the earth, plants and trees. Hereof one herb is hot, another cold, another dry and yet another moist, one astringent, one laxative, some corrosive and others venomous. So, diverse herbs have diverse qualities.

3. It comes about that if it helps one disease, by and by it hinders another, for everything works according to its properties whenas is there made separation in the body. And of this separation is engendered bloud and other humours. They are just like gunpouder in that so long as they sit still, there comes no harm therefrom. But if it be brought to the fire, it will at once demonstrate its secret nature and is kindled with a destructive fire. A fire which cannot be quenched with water, for the cold and dry, hot and moist, strive among themselves, a wind is stirred up that breaks all things near it. The same thing happens with Honie, that when it comes to the area of the Liver, it separates there and shows its nature to pass up and swell with wind. It is no surprise then, that the veins of the Liver can be broken by contention. When this occurs, Imposthumes are created in different places and causes such inflammations that the veins break easily. Although many highly recommend Honie, these are not Philosophers nor do they understand the nature of it. But when it is prepared as a Simple, fixed as Wine, then it is the most potent of Medicines among the Vegetals. There is nothing like it.

Give God thanks and be generous to the poor. The dosage of this is one grain and it must be taken morning and night on an empty stomach until the disease is gone. Now Praise God.

a) Clarify the honey

ESSENCE OF HONEY

Although this recipe describes the Essence of Honey we thought it a fitting place to mention this work:

Take of Honey well despumated[1] as much as you please, pour upon it as much of the best rectified spirit of Wine as will cover it five or six fingers breadth, digest them in a glass vessel well closed (the fourth part only being full) in a temperate BALNEO the space of a fortnight, or till the spirit be very well tinged, then decant off the spirit, and put on more till all the tincture be extracted, then put all these tinctures together, and evaporate the spirit till what remains begin to be thickish at the bottom, and of a golden colour.

This is a very excellent Essence of Honey, and is of so pleasant an odour, that scarce any thing is like to it. It is so cordial, that it even revives the dying, if two or three drops thereof be taken in some cordial water.

1 To 'clarify' or remove the scum from the surface.

b) Pour into a circulatory vessel, in this instance we chose a long necked flask

c) Add strong rectified spirit of wine

d) Having been taken out of the incubator; most Alchemists suggest a philosophical month, that is, 40 days.

e) Separate

 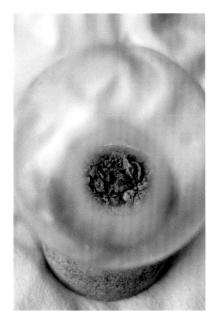

a) Having gathered our blood we placed the material in an incubator for 40 days by which time some of it had clotted like liver. We added spirit of wine and returned to the incubator.

b) The caput mortum of blood having the let the eagle fly seven times.

QUINTESSENCE OF BLOOD

There is a very great balsam in blood, says Paracelsus, comparable to Aurum Potabile. We find an interesting recipe for the quintessence of blood in the *Aurora Chymica*, a short tract covering various works on animals.

Take the blood of very sound and healthy young men, in the spring time, Mercury being above the horizon and in conjunction with the Sun in Gemini or Virgo: Take of such blood a large quantity, gather it in glass vessels, let it settle some time, until it hath thrown out all its waterish humour, which separate by wary inclination; Take now of this concrete blood, five or six pounds, which put to ten or twelve pints of well rectified Spirit of Wine in a fit vessel, shake them very well dissolved and diluted by the

c) Distil carefully and return the distillate over the body.

d) The resultant essence. We shall calcinate the body, wash the salts and gently dry before returning the essence to the body. Having distilled the liquid we noted traces of salt resting on the surface of the liquid, showing us we had volatized at least some of the salts. Once the essence has been returned to the body we place it in an incubator.

Spirit of Wine; shut well the vessel and let it so digest six or eight days in warm ashes (but have a care your heat be not so great as to Coagulate the blood), your digestion being over, put to your distilling vessel its head and distil with gentle fire; separate so the spirit of wine, change then your receiver, increasing gradually your fire until the distillation be fully over; which being done, increase your fire until the volatile salt arise in the head of the alembick as white as snow, keep well this salt and add it to the white liquor before distilled, but first rectify that liquor, and then add the salt and rectify both yet several times; to these thus purified add the fixed salt drawn out of the *caput mortuum* of the blood, by calcination, solution, filtration and coagulation and these oftentimes repeated, having made conjunction of these purified substances digest them for some days, then separate by gentle distillation the phlegm; what shall remain behind is the Arcanum of blood, and a most noble Quintessence.

The author goes on to say: 'It is a very high balsam excelling much the power and virtue of Natural Balsam, both in preserving from corruption and also in healing all wounds, ulcers etc. A potent preservative in time of pestilence, leprosie, palsie and gout of all sorts, in certainty it gives present ease to and radically cures; to hectical and ptisical persons a certain refuge; the quantane and all kinds of mellencholly it perfectly helps. Wounds and ulcers both internal and external, it in short time perfectly conglatinates, and radically dries up, even to admiration. It may not without benefit be made use of in all or most diseases; it is to be taken in vegiles suitable to the distemper, if to be had if not in broth, cinnamon, or treacle water and with a fasting stomach.'

The Plant Stone of Hollandus

This Agent is the Form that Matter wanted.   – EIRENÆUS PHILALETHES

Although we have already made mention of him, among the greatest alchemists stands Johann Isaac Hollandus. The works he has left us are treasures, being clearer and more concise than other authors and those interested in the Art will do well to study them. We will consider Hollandus again in our book on menstruums, but for now we will examine his work *Opera Vegetabile* and reveal some of the secrets it holds.

Perhaps the most notable contribution Hollandus offers in this work is the means by which we draw forth the Sal Ammoniac: 'because,' says he, 'the spirit of all things is Sal Ammoniac. That is why Sal Ammoniac is designated and pictured as the Sun. For the Sun is the supreme sign and the most powerful planet of heaven…and is a wondrous thing because without it nothing in alchemy can be brought to perfection.' This is our Mercurius, our Spirit, which we have aimed to capture in our previous works by macerating the herb using the Spirit of Wine. He observes that every herb has this Spirit, but depending on whether the herb is Hot or Cold, will relinquish more or less:

> One kind of Ammoniac does not make the same sort of projection from one species or one kind of herb. Such, however, is the fault of the laboratory worker who has made the Ammoniac. (It means) that he has not purified it well enough and has not drawn it off often enough. For he who would make the Ammoniac correctly, must draw it off and off, often, till nothing remains and it becomes as white as snow.

Sal ammoniac passing into the receiver

Every plant, mineral and metal has this Spirit and each Spirit: 'has a miraculous power and virtue for a special sickness; and each spirit has the power to accomplish some special work with the help of other species, as well in metals as in human beings, for God has created all things on behalf of man.' But this Spirit, being locked in a body made of the four elements, is corrupted and unable to break from its earthly tomb. 'In addition,' says he, 'the time of the world is up, and it is now becoming too old and weak. The sun and the elements are losing their power, and the elements are becoming so infected and impure so that the spirits, on account of the impurity of the elements, can only have an insignificant curative effect... If now they would still manifest their powers as they did long ago, human beings would still live today into their 200 years and beyond, and they would in everything have the same powers as they had previously; although people are now also weak and delicate and could not tolerate the spirits of the herbs as if they still had the powers of years ago. They would certainly have to take and use them tempered. If they did that, they would live even much longer and stay younger.'

> That is why all herbs and other things have to be killed, annihilated and reduced to powder and ashes[1] and finally to water. Afterwards, the soul, or spirit, has to be infused back into them and a perfect body must be made of them. Then you have an earthly treasure that is better than gold and silver and precious stones. For you have a perfect glorified corpus (body) which will never pass away but will last eternally, passing through all things. And where it passes through, it will not leave any corruption or disease at all, but it will heal that through which it penetrates before leaving it.[2]

'Likewise,' he relates, 'I gave it to twelve lepers. They were so leprous that they could not be recognised at all. Within nine days they became healthy and good looking like a newborn child, although one could still see the scars where the

---

1   He goes onto say: 'In addition, my child, you must know: The fact that I said in the previous chapter that one must kill and let the herbs die, and make a powder or ashes of them, is to be understood as follows. One must draw off the evil, impure humidity, or let the herbs dry of themselves, which is best.' *Opera Vegetabile*, chapter VI.

2   'Not only will it make it (the body) healthy,' continues he, 'healthier than it had ever been, and it will also keep it healthy from then on. Yes, if it had never been healthy before it would be made healthy thereby and preserved. That is why I may well say that it is above all earthly treasures.'

lepra had been bad. Within a month those had also disappeared by taking as much of the quintessence as was equivalent to the weight of a grain of wheat. Also, I have given it to about one hundred persons on their deathbed. They had already been given up by the physicians who said that they were to die and that it was impossible for them to live one more day. I gave them the quintessence and brought them back to health within 24 hours. Thereupon, I gave them a *Confortative*, and they went outside again within 8 days. They said they had not been as healthy during all of their lifetime, and they thought they were flying when they were walking.'

And a little later he writes: 'And further, if a man were to take everyday a little of the quintessence in wine, with his food and drink, or in the morning, he would not die, unless nature would die of its own. He would remain in the same being-ness and condition as he was when he began taking the quintessence, and his face would not get older nor his members more awkward, stiff or bent, because the quintessence would drive out right in the beginning the evil which man might have within him. For wherever the quintessence gets, no infirmity or evil can remain. That is why it is called quintessence or elixir. As soon as it has consumed or driven away the sickness, it makes the blood youthful again. When then the blood has been rejuvenated, all members again become well, quick and strong and remain always so. Neither need he be afraid of any kind of poison, for no poison can harm such a man.'

In the tract we're discussing, Hollandus offers a number of recipes, each differing in perfection and each revealing a different mode of preparing the Earth, the Air, the Fire and the Water. It is only when these are finally recombined that we create the quintessence.

Let us consider the practical work. We placed freshly gathered seeds of Angelica in an alembic and hermetically sealed our system before proceeding with a gentle heat. All herbs have within them the four elements, but one is invisible: Air. By applying a gentle heat we will sweat off the water, allowing the air to rise.

To that end you must separate the water from the air, the earth and the fire. Then you must separate the air and the fire from the earth and purify the air. Fire in itself is pure, but fire must be worked upon together with the air, by means of the air that is in the fire. Then purify the air by calcination, as I have taught before and shall teach still better later on.

The Air is the sal ammoniac (which he sometimes calls spirit and sometimes calls Mercurius) and the Fire is the essential oil of the plant. In my experience some plants release the Water, then the Air and finally the Fire, but in others, the water comes first, then the fire and then the air. In this instance the water came first and then the essential oil or fire. It was only by increasing the heat that the sal ammoniac finally rose in the alembic and fastened itself about the helm in beautiful ice-like crystals of a golden yellow colour.

We now have our Water and Fire in the receiver, the Air in the helm of the alembic and the unprepared Earth in the boiling flask. This is what Hollandus has to say regarding the next step:

> When now the air, or the white spirit, has been drawn over cleanly in such a way, you must heat stronger for another 12 hours, increasing every four hours; still stronger for 20 hours; and as strong as you can during the last four hours, so that the barrel stands in the heat. The oil will go over within that time, mixed with the air, or whatever it is to be called. Then you have to draw the three elements from the earth.

In the following chapter of his work he then begins to describe 'from what the pure glorified corpus is made.' It is here that the confusion begins in earnest, his language becomes obscure and he leaves much to the imagination. Firstly, he advises us to separate the oil and keep it aside before purifying the spirit:

> After you have removed the oil, put the spirit into an alembic; put a head and a receiver on it. Distill it with a temperate fire, that is, not too hot and not too cold. When you have distilled it, add the feces that have stayed in the alembic to the earth in order to calcinate them together. Put the spirit back into the alembic, put the head on it and the receptacle. Distill as you did at first. Thus, you must distill over and over ten times. Then the spirit, which was before poisonous, hard, evil, sharp and useless to anyone, becomes pleasingly sweet and natural. Now, however, it is pleasing, good and natural, so that its virtue cannot be described or explained. That is the fat spirit I mean when the pure, dry CORPUS is to be fattened.

He advises us to wash the Earth with 'burnt wine,' but we chose to wash it with its own water before preparing it according to art.

> Therefore, when you have drawn all the elements from the earth, put the earth into a long earthenware vessel, baked out of potter's earth, so that it gets heated through all the better. Put it into the furnace of calcination, and calcinate it for three days and three nights in as much heat and strong fire as you can give. When the three days are over, take it out of the vessel and put it on a stone. Rub it firmly with brandy ('burnt wine') out of the vessel. After that, put it into a glass barrel, pour more of the wine upon it, and place the vessel into the Bath till the earth is dissolved. But cork your glass well to prevent the spirit of the brandy from flying out; since the spirit is altogether too agile and too subtle, it would fly away invisibly.

What follows is a lengthy process of solve et coagula, whereby he frequently dissolves the salts in brandy, pours off the alcohol, distils and recohabits repeating the process until you have a 'very clear white.'

> He will take away all combustible fattiness[1] and dry the marrow of all the bones and members without obesity. And GOD will fill the tubes of the poor, the thighs and the skull, with fat spirit. That is the fattiness which the transfigured bodies receive after the soul again enters the pure body. Then it is one (thing) and they will never again part from each other. It is one thing. The body is spirit; and the spirit, body. Then it is fixed and one quintessence.

The bones he is referring to are the *sal salis* which we will extract shortly, the combustible fattiness is the essential oil and the fat spirit is the Air or sal ammoniac which we need to gather from the helm.

We chose to change the flask containing the Earth and add a clean flask with a 150ml of spirit of wine, well rectified. We then sealed the system and with a gentle heat we 'washed' the helm of the alembic and collected our sal ammoniac which came over with the alcohol. This liquid now contained the mercurial nature of the plant which we circulated with our Fire, the essential oil. Having

1 'That is the fat spirit,' he tells us, 'I mean when the pure, dry CORPUS is to be fattened.'

a) The Earth, the Air, the Fire and the Water
   first separated

b) Once we have separated the Fire and Water
   we wash the Earth with the Water

c) The Fire and Water before separation

d) Washing of the Earth

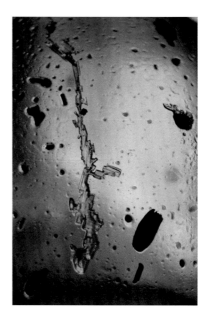

e) The Air

f) Distilling the Fire

done this we placed the dark brown liquid in a retort to distil.[1] 'When,' says he, 'the earth is thus dissolved in its own spirit, as I have taught before, and becomes fixed with it, it does ten thousand things where before it did one.'

Having distilled the alcohol over, keep aside and change flasks. The Fire will now pass over, golden and clear and smelling less burnt, keep aside and raise the heat to drive the remaining Air over. Pour the alcohol into the boiling flask, give a gentle heat and repeat the process. You will now have the essential oil and the spirit or alcohol containing the Air or mercurial vibrations.

Whilst the above is distilling, let us take our Earth, which we prepared from the dead body of the plant earlier.

Then you have to draw the three elements from the earth. First, the water, then the air, and following that, the oil or fire. Now you must calcinate the earth in an even heat for three days and three nights. Give a strong fire, as hot and strong as you can. Then take it out, and you will have the earth pure and clean. After this also purify the air and the fire, and give it its water, pure and clean. That is the vinegar or brandy ('burnt wine'), well cleansed and purified by distillation, as I taught you previously. Now, put the four elements together and make of them a perfect Corpus. Now the elements are again gathered and united with each other, joined and fixed. Now it is a perfect glorified body which lasts imperishably into eternity. If now all artists who were ever born, or may yet be born, would come together, they could never again separate the elements from each other. Yes, all the devils in hell now have no power to do that, neither anyone else but GOD alone. Only now may you say that you have the quintessence, which is indeed a gift of GOD.

At which point Hollandus falls silent, leaving how we are to fix the elements for further recipes later in the work, of which he gives a number; one of which, interestingly, does not admit the essential oil, only working with the sal ammoniac and the salt. He does, however, close with the following words, a process we should be familiar with having considered the work on elixirs:

---

1   In his first recipe for the Quintessence he says: 'It is here not required that the elements be divided from each other, each alone in a special way, but only to cleanse and purify them.'

The purified Earth

Concerning the earth of which I said previously that you must again draw
off the brandy that is good. Draw it off and do as I have taught you here.
But it would be better if you were to pour the brandy back upon the earth
and distill it off again; then pour it on again, as I have taught until now.
And this so often till the whole quantity of the distilled wine were again infused into the earth, and you would again dissolve it, that is the CORPUS,
in a good other brandy and put it again into the Bath, as you did at first;
and again distill the brandy off, and pour it on again till it had sucked in
everything; and dissolve it again as at first. And if you did this the fourth
time, the earth would become so strong that it could not be described; neither could its virtues be expressed. When the earth is thus dissolved in its
own spirit, as I have taught before, and becomes fixed with it, it does then
ten thousand things where before it did one. This glorified CORPUS, or
quintessence, prepared in this way, no King could pay with all his wealth
for one pound of it, so great is its strength and virtue. Blessed is he who has

Imbibe the Air and the Fire with the Earth and feed with Spirit

it, and things will go well for him who uses it well. But he who misuses it will be tormented by GOD temporarily in this life and eternally in the next.

Like many alchemists he takes us so far, but leaves us to make our own inquiry. Simply reading the texts will not suffice, it is only when we embark upon experiment that the matter can be resolved.

Since we had very little salt, having leached the ashes with distilled water twice before calcinating them, we proceeded by joining the Fire to the Earth and slowly feeding with the Air, which we dripped carefully into the flask before sealing and incubating. We repeated the process of moistening our earth with our mercury and sealing.

An alchemist could spend a lifetime working on Hollandus alone and we will meet him again before we are through, but for now, we must end our inquiry into the fixed quintessence of Hollandus.

The Plant Phoenix

We now step into the occult shadows of Alchemy and the work described as Palingenesis (from the Greek *palin*, again, and *genesis*, birth); the resurrection of a dead plant from its ashes.[1] It is an area neglected or forgotten and yet, the pursuit of the Plant Phoenix offers a priceless contribution to the deeper understanding of our art. Therefore we introduce this area of alchemical lore and hope to inspire the gentle reader with the immense rewards this work promises. After all, some would regard the ability to transmute the most stalwart of atheists, a worthier quest than to merely transmute base metals.

Our subject was much discussed by Plato, Seneca, Erastus, Avicenna, Albertus Magnus, Cornelius Agrippa, Eckartshausen and W.B. Yeats, to name but a few. Indeed, the art of regeneration was both the keystone to the Egyptian rites and central to the sacred Mysteries of Eleusis in which the myth of Persephone takes pride of place.

In terms of evidence we have many witnesses attesting to the truth of this procedure. In 1687, in the presence of Queen Christina of Sweden, Kircher resurrected a rose from its ashes:

> M. Joseph du Chesne... affirmes that himselfe saw an excellent Polish Physician of Cracovia, who kept in Glasses, the Ashes of almost all the Hearbs that are knowne... he tooke that where the Ashes of a Rose were preserved; and holding it over a lighted Candle, so soone as ever it began to feel the Heat, you should presently see the Ashes begin to Move; which afterwards

1 We should note that he leaves recipes to resurrect birds, which we will shortly cover.

rising up, and dispersing themselves about the Glasse, you should immediately observe a kind of little Dark Cloud; which dividing it selfe into many parts it came at length to represent a Rose; but so faire, so fresh, and so perfect a one, that you would have thought it to have been as substantial and as odoriferous a Rose, as any that growes on the Rose-tree.[1]

Throughout Paracelsus's work we hear him describe all living things as having a material and sidereal body. Matter, he says, is merely 'coagulated smoke' bound to the universal Spirit by an intermediate link, which owes itself to this Spirit. 'This intermediate link between matter and spirit belongs to all three kingdoms of nature. In the mineral kingdom it is called Stannar or Trughat, in the vegetable kingdom Leffas; and it forms, in connection with the vital force of the vegetable kingdom, the Primum Ens, which possesses the highest medicinal properties.'[2]

In this way the Primum Ens or First Entity attracts its etheric or sidereal essence and by using a quickening heat, the plant appears resurrected from its ashes and thus the form may be made to 'appear and disappear.'

'For "if,"' continues our guide in his *De Resucitationibus*, 'a thing loses its material substance, the invisible form still remains in the light of nature (the astral light); and if we can re-clothe that form with visible matter, we may make that form visible again. All matter is composed of three elements – sulphur, mercury and salt. By alchemical means we may create a magnetic attraction in the astral form, so that it may attract from the elements (the Ākāśa) those principles which it possessed before its mortification, and incorporate them and become visible again.'

It (the seminal part) will restore the coarse part, or rather its own coarse part, purged of filth to the extent it deserves, for when the world is liquefied by fires and heat joins homogenous things together, kindred things which retain the traces of similar motions will also come together.[3]

---

1 Gaffarel, Jacques, *Unheard-of Curiosities.* Translated by Edmund Chilmead, London 1650.
2 Hartmann, 1896.
3 Leibniz, O*n the Resurrection of Bodies.* Quoted from Lloyd Strickland's essay: 'Leibniz, the "Flower of Substance" and the Resurrection of the Same Body" in *The Philosophical Forum*, volume 40, issue 3, 2009.

Quite apart from unveiling the mystery of resurrection, palingenesis allows us to approach our sidereal nature whilst proving the immortality of the Soul. Palingenesis is the means by which the psychic vitality of the soul, impressing upon the Astral Light, can be attracted to its body through analogy, for by the authority of the Soul, or Astral Form, the physical matrix is informed and organised to appear like a wraith in a glass.

'In this way,' adds Paracelsus, 'it often happens that the power of a first entity of this kind may be enclosed in a glass, and be brought to such condition that the form of that herb grows of itself without any earth, and even when it has quite grown it has no body, but something shaped like a body, the cause of which is that it has no liquid of the earth. Hence it happens that its stem is nothing more than a mere apparition to the sight, because it can be again rubbed down to a juice by the finger, just like smoke, which shews a substantial form but is not perceptible by any sense of touch.'

Naturally little has been left of the process and we are unaware of any present day success in this field, but what is of interest, from the meagre crumbs we have, is the similarity of approach they partake in.

Below is a recipe from John French's *Art of Distillation*:

Take the whole herb with flowers and roots and make it very clean. Then bruise it in a stone mortar and put it into a large glass vessel so two parts of three may be empty. Cover it exceeding close and let it stand in putrefaction in a moderate heat the space of half a year, and it will all be turned into a water.

Take the foregoing water and distill it in a gourd glass (the joints being well closed) in ashes, and there will come forth a water and an oil and in the upper part of the vessel will hang a volatile salt. Separate the oil from the water and keep it by itself. With the water purify the volatile salt by dissolving, filtering, and coagulating. The salt being thus purified, imbibe with the said oil until it will imbibe no more. Digest them well together for a month in a vessel hermetically sealed. And by this means you shall have a most subtle essence, which being held over a gentle heat will fly up into the glass and represent the perfect idea of that vegetable whereof it is the essence.

The process of resurrecting a plant is elucidated further by Franz Hartmann:

If we would burn a tree, and enclose the ashes and the smoke and the vapour, and all the elements that made up the tree into a great bottle and plant
a living seed of that tree into the ashes, we might resurrect the same kind of
a tree again out of its ashes because there would be a centre of life, to which
all the elements that were before necessary to form that tree could be again
attracted to form another tree of the same kind, having all the characteristics
of the former; but if there were no seed, there would be no tree, because
the character of the tree is neither in the ashes nor in the vapour nor in the
smoke, but in the *Mysterium magnum*, the eternal storehouse of life, from
which it may be attracted again by a seed, and be made to live in a new form
endowed with greater virtues and powers than the ones it possessed before.[1]

Note Hartmann's use of the plant seed to quicken the body; in this respect and
in other accounts the use of moonlight in the operation is of importance, very
little differs from the process. The following, and perhaps most interesting example, is a receipt from Ebenezer Sibly:

Take any whole herb, or flower, with its root, make it very clean, and bruise
it in a stone mortar quite small; then put it into a glass vessel hermetically
sealed; but be sure the vessel be two parts in three empty. Then place it
for putrefaction in a gentle heat in balneo, not more than blood warm, for
six months, by which it will be all resolved into water. Take this water,
and pour it into a glass retort, and place a receiver thereunto, the joints of
which must be well closed; distil it into a sand-heat until there come forth
a water and an oil; and in the upper part of the vessel will hang a volatile
salt. Separate the oil from the water, and keep it by itself, but with the water
purify the volatile salt by dissolving, filtering, and coagulating. When the
salt is thus purified, imbibe with it the said oil, until it is well combined.
Then digest them well together for a month in a vessel hermetically sealed;
and by this means will be obtained a most subtile essence, which being held
over a gentle heat of a candle, the spirit will fly up into the glass where it
is confined, and represent the perfect idea or similitude of that vegetable
whereof it is the essence: and in this manner will that thin substance, which
is like impalpable ashes or salt, send forth from the bottom of the glass the

1 Hartmann, 1896.

manifest form of whatever herb it is the *menstruum*, in perfect vegetation, growing by little and little, and putting on so fully the form of stalks, leaves, and flowers, in full and perfect appearance, that any one would believe the same to be natural and corporeal; though at the same time it is nothing more than the spiritual idea endued with a spiritual essence. This shadowed figure, as soon as the vessel is taken from the heat or candle, returns to its *caput mortuum*, or ashes, again, and vanishes away like an apparition, becoming a chaos, or confused matter.[2]

If we compare the work on the quintessence and the above account, the process is very similar; the volatile salts Sibly refers to are the 'Sal Ammoniac' revealed by Johann Isaac Hollandus.

It is interesting to note that Sibly seems to declare that this 'most subtile essence' is in fact the 'magnet' to which the character or soul, of the plant, is drawn. A short, but no less interesting, receipt can be found in Sloane MS 633 which suggests the use of dew:

Gather May dew, and set it to putrefy in a close glass; then distill it, and out of the feces extract a salt according to Art. Take this salt 1 ounce and out of the distilled water, 2 pints.

What herbs you would see, take a handful or two of their seed and powder it; and pour on it the water so much as the water may remain three fingers higher than the seed that lies in it, and put the salt and distilled water of dew and the seeds together, into a strong glass and lute it or seal it hermetically; (N.B. The glass must be high enough to take the representation of the plant). Then set it in your Chamber where is clear light. And in the night when the moon clearly shines in, when it is bad weather. Secure your bottle and so keep thus till it is dry.

And when you please to see the flowers and the plant you must set the glass in a little warm sand and so in a moment; as it were comes the plant and flowers up. And when you take the heat away the flower and the plant goes.

2 *A New and Complete Illustration of the Celestial Science of Astrology: or, The Art Of Foretelling Future Events and Contingencies by the Aspects, Positions, Influences and of Heavenly Bodies.* PART IV, p. 1114–1115, 1826.

Paracelsus's claims of regeneration did not end with plants, and although his references are piecemeal, we shall leave you a rather strange recipe for the regeneration of birds:

> And here something more is to be noticed. If the living bird be burned to dust and ashes in a sealed cucurbite with the third degree of fire, and then, still shut up, be putrefied with the highest degree of putrefaction in a *venter equinus* so as to become a mucilaginous phlegm, then that phlegm can be brought to maturity, and so, renovated and restored, can become a living bird, provided the phlegm be once more enclosed in its jar or receptacle. This is to revive the dead by regeneration and clarification, which is indeed a great and profound miracle of Nature. By this process all birds can be killed and again made to live, to be renovated and restored. This is the very greatest and highest miracle and mystery of God, which God has disclosed to mortal man. For you must know that in this way men can be generated without natural father and mother; that is to say, not in the natural way from the woman, but by art and industry of a skilled Spagyrist a man can be born and grow, as will hereafter be described.[1]

Finally, another recipe for the restoration of birds comes from *The Art of Distillation*:

> A bird is restored to life thus. Take a bird and put it alive into a gourd glass and seal it hermetically. Burn it to ashes in the third degree of fire. Then putrefy it in horse dung into a mucilaginous phlegm. So, by a continued digestion that phlegm must be brought to a further maturity (being taken out and put into an oval vessel of a just bigness to hold it) by an exact digestion, and will become a renewed bird which, says Paracelsus, is one of the greatest wonders of nature, and shows the great virtue of putrefaction.

So we conclude our inquiry on the art of palingenesis.

1 Waite, A.E., 1967 (volume I).

The Homunculus

Human beings may come into existence without natural parents. That is to say, such beings grow without being developed and born by a female organism; by the art of an experienced spagyricus.

– PARACELSUS

To the alchemists, the creation myths of old held the key to man's first beginnings; to the ancients, if man, born of the earth and quickened from the breath of God, or made from the ashes of the Titans, or Osiris, reincarnated like the Nazarene, was substantial, then he could therefore be substantiated.

By searching into their very being the alchemists finally discovered that man was not just a creature perpetuating his own species or kind, but was capable of an altogether other means of generation, of anthropomorphic elementals,[1] golems and homunculi.

In his works Paracelsus distinguishes between two types of homunculi, and although we are primarily interested in the generation of species through Art, we shall illustrate his lesser homunculus, which is said to preserve man from unfavourable heavenly influences.

'We neither wish nor are able to hinder the course of the heavenly bodies,' notes our Master, 'yet we have the power of resisting them, just as a strong wall can be assailed with bombardment and with engines. The sun impresses its influence on a stone. If that stone be thrown into the water, the sun can no longer bring its powers to bear on it, and thus the stone is preserved.'[2]

---

1 We must distinguish between *Elementaries* and *Elementals*; the first are beings inhabiting the elements, the second are thought-forms created by the imagination of man. We have purposely bypassed this area of Paracelsian philosophy since it is simply too big for these pages, but I would strongly encourage students eager to pursue this line of Paracelsian thinking to explore his own words on the matter as well as researching other works, most especially Franz Bardon's *Initiation into Hermetics*.

2 Waite, A.E., 1967.

In *A Book Concerning Long Life* he continues: 'If Mars should be disposed to destroy me, and there be a mental inclination from him in my mind, which might induce mental disease, I construct my Homunculus, that the operation of Mars may be directed to this image, and I may get off safely. It is easier to affect the Homunculus, and so the planet is able to work its will more gently and without resistance. It takes the easier course, and leaves the more difficult one.'

In this instance, and where a person wishes to protect from incantations, one would create a homunculus from wax, using one's mumia in the figure.

Against incantations, too, we would prescribe something, so that a long life may not be taken away by means of these. Remedies of this kind we have mentioned in several places, not as conservations, but simply for a cure of incantations. But the same is to be understood concerning them as in the case of the malefic stars. Incantations, that is, are to be guarded against in the same way as mental influences transferred to a homunculus. A similar operation holds good in its reversal to that which binds our minds and mental organs and our beings, the seat whereof is in the mind, as we remark in our treatise on incantations. It must be directed to some other subject, and not to that which we have from the stars, but to its own incantation in the following manner: I construct a homunculus of wax to serve my purpose, and this I put in its place. Then, whatever attempt is made against me by way of incantation will be fulfilled on this image. For that proceeds from my mind, & the incantation from his mind, so that the minds meet, and on neither side is any harm done, or any effect produced. Under this form we have made clear the mode of resisting and preventing incantations by means of images.

Accounts of creating the mandragore[1] from the sperm of a hanged man and incubating it in a hen's eggs are infrequent, but Agrippa seems familiar with the work when he discloses the following: 'and there is an art wherewith by a hen sitting upon eggs may be generated a form like to a man, which I have seen and know how to make, which magicians say hath in it wonderful virtues, and this they call the true mandrake.'

1 One is a thought form using living essence of the mandrake as a focus and bred on blood and milk to determine the resulting familiar to the parent; the other is said to be a physical living being with highly actuated awareness or spiritual consciousness.

An homunculus made of wax and mumia

This mandragore was most often fed on milk and blood and when matured was said to protect its parent and was considered a luck charm:

> Thus the author of the *Secrets du Petit Albert* (Lyons 1718) says that a peasant had a Bryonia root of human shape, which he received from a gipsy. He buried it at a lucky conjunction of the Moon with Venus in spring, and on a Monday, in a grave, and then sprinkled it with milk in which three field-mice had been drowned. In a month it became more human-like than ever. Then he placed it in an oven with Vervain, wrapped it afterwards in a dead man's shroud, and so long as he kept it, he never failed in luck at games or work.[1]

As alchemists we wish to discuss the possibility of creating a living homunculus under laboratory conditions and therefore we must return to our guide: 'But neither,' he writes, 'must we by any means forget the generation of homunculi. For there is some truth in this thing, although for a long time it was held in a most occult manner and with secrecy, while there was no little doubt and question among some of the old philosophers, whether it was possible to Nature and Art, that a man should be begotten without the female body and the natural womb. I answer hereto, that it is in no way opposed to spagyric art, and to Nature, nay, that it is perfectly possible.' The word homunculus means 'little man.' Paracelsus, describing him further, tells us:

> The necromancers call it the Abreo; the philosophers name such creatures naturals, and they are commonly called Mandragoræ. Still, error prevails on this subject through the chaos in which certain persons have involved the true use of the homunculus. Its origin is in the sperm. By means of complete digestion, which takes place in a venter equinus, a homunculus is generated like in all respects, in body, blood, principal and inferior members, to him from whom is issued.[2]

What we have in way of receipts are few and far between. Accounts are even rarer, but we do hear of the Count von Kueffstein, of Tyrol, in the year 1775, who

1 See Friend, Rev. Hilderic, *Flowers and Flower Lore*, W. Sonnenschein & Co. London, 1884.
2 Paracelsus, *A Book Concerning Long Life*, Book the Second, Ch. IV: 'Concerning Pearls.'

created a number of 'spirits' which he kept in bottles. Evidence comes from Masonic manuscripts and prints and the diary of the Count's butler, Jas. Kammerer. We are told that the Count and an Italian mystic, Abbé Geloni, prepared ten 'prophesying spirits' within five weeks. These had the form of 'a king, a queen, a knight, a monk, a nun, an architect, a miner, a seraph, and finally of a blue and a red spirit,' and were kept in large bottles; the story runs thus:[3]

> The bottles were closed with ox-bladders, and with a great magic seal (Solomon's Seal?). The spirits swam about in those bottles and were about one span long, and the Count was very anxious that they should grow. They were therefore buried under two cartloads of horse manure, and the pile daily sprinkled with a certain liquor prepared with great trouble by the two adepts and made out of some 'very disgusting materials.' The pile of manure began after such sprinklings to ferment and to steam as if heated by a subterranean fire, and at least once every three days, when everything was quiet, at the approach of the night, the two gentlemen would leave the convent and go to pray and to fumigate at that pile of manure. After the bottles were removed the 'spirits' had grown to be each one about one and a half span long, so that the bottles were almost too small to contain them, and the male homunculi had come into possession of heavy beards, and the nails. By some means the Abbé Schiloni provided them with appropriate clothing, each one according to his rank and dignity. In the bottle of the red and in that of the blue spirit, however, there was nothing to be seen but 'clear water'; but whenever the Abbé knocked three times at the seal upon the mouth of the bottles, speaking at the same time some Hebrew words, the water in the bottle began to turn blue (respectively red) and the blue and the red spirits would show their faces, first very small, but growing in proportions until they assumed the size of an ordinary human face. The face of the blue spirit was beautiful, like an angel, but that of the red one bore a horrible expression.
>
> These beings were fed by the Count about once every three or four days with some rose-coloured substance which he kept in a silver box, and of which he gave to each spirit a pill about the size of a pea. Once every week the water had to be removed, and the bottles filled again with pure rain-wa-

3 Hartmann, 1896.

ter. This change had to be accomplished very rapidly, because during the few moments that the sprits were exposed to the air they closed their eyes, and seemed to become weak and unconscious, as if they were about to die. But the blue spirit was never fed, nor was the water changed; while the red one received once a week a thimbleful of fresh blood of some animal (chicken), and this blood disappeared in the water as soon as it was poured into it, without colouring or troubling it. The water containing the red spirit had to be changed once every two or three days. As soon as the bottle was opened it become dark and cloudy and emitted an odour of rotten eggs.

In the course of time these spirits grew to be about two spans long and their bottles were now almost too small for them to stand erect: the Count therefore provided them with appropriate seats. These bottles were carried to the place where the Masonic Lodge of which the Count was the presiding Master met, and after each meeting they were carried back again. During the meetings the Spirits gave prophecies about future events that usually proved to be correct. They knew the most secret things, but each of them was only acquainted with such things as belonged to his station: for instance, the King could talk politics, the monk about religion, the miner about minerals, &c.; but the blue and the red spirits seemed to know everything. (Some facts proving their clairvoyant powers are given in the original.)

By some accident the glass containing the monk fell one day upon the floor, and was broken. The poor monk died after a few painful respirations, in spite of all the efforts of the Count to save his life, and his body was buried in the garden. An attempt to generate another one, made by the Count without the assistance of the Abbé, who had left, resulted in a failure, as it produced only a small thing like a leech, which had very little vitality, and soon died.

One day the King escaped from his bottle, which had not been properly sealed, and was found by Kammerer sitting on the top of the bottle containing the Queen, attempting to scratch with his nails the seal away, and to liberate her. In answer to the servant's call for help, the Count rushed in, and after a prolonged chase caught the King, who, from his long exposure to the air and the want of his appropriate element, had become faint, and was replaced into his bottle - not, however, without succeeding to scratch the nose of the Count.

This story contains many elements that will be instructive to the student of alchemy or magic, and can be compared with profit to the grimoire accounts.

To create a living homunculus Paracelsus leaves us with these, no doubt incomplete, instructions:[1]

> Let the semen of a man putrefy by itself in a sealed curcubite with the highest putrefaction of the *venter equinus* for forty days, or until it begins at last to live, move, and be agitated, which can easily be seen. After this time it will be in some degree like a human being, but, nevertheless, transparent and without body. If now, after this, it be every day nourished and fed cautiously and prudently with the arcanum of human blood, and kept for forty weeks in the perpetual and equal heat of a *venter equinus*, it becomes, thenceforth a true and living infant, having all the members of a child that is born from a woman, but much smaller. This we call a homunculus; and it should be afterwards educated with the greatest care and zeal, until it grows up and begins to display intelligence. Now, this is one of the greatest secrets which God has revealed to mortal and fallible man. It is a miracle and marvel of God, an arcanum above all arcana, and deserves to be kept secret until the last times, when there shall be nothing hidden, but all things shall be made manifest.[2]

In *The Art of Distillation*, John French leaves an allegorical account of the process:

> Take the best wheat and the best wine, of each a like quantity. Put them into a glass which you must hermetically seal. Then let them putrefy in horse dung three days, or until the wheat begins to germinate or to sprout forth, which then must be taken forth and bruised in a mortar and be pressed through a linen cloth. There will come forth a white juice like milk. You must cast away the feces. Let this juice be put into a glass, which must not be above half full. Stop it close and set it in horse dung as before for the

---

1 Waite, A.E., 1967.

2 He goes onto say: 'Although up to this time it has not been known to men, it was, nevertheless, known to the wood-sprites and nymphs and giants long ago, because they themselves were sprung from this source.'

space of fifty days. If the heat be temperate, and not exceeding the natural heat of man, the matter will be turned into a spagyrical blood and flesh, like an embryo. This is the principal and next matter out of which is generated a two-fold sperm, viz., of the father and mother generating the homunculus, without which there can be made no generation, whether human or animal.

From the blood and flesh of this embryo let the water be separated in balneum, and the air in ashes, and both be kept by themselves. Then to the feces of the latter distillation, let the water of the former distillation be added, both which must (the glass being close stopped) putrefy in balneum the space of ten days. After this, distill the water a second time (which is then the vehiculum of the fire) together with the fire, in ashes. Then distill off this water in a gentle balneum, and in the bottom remains the fire which must be distilled in ashes. Keep both these apart. And thus you have the four elements separated from the chaos of the embryo.

The feculent earth is to be reverberated in a close vessel for the space of four days. In the interim, distill off the fourth part of the first distillation in balneum and cast it away. The other three parts distill in ashes, and pour it upon the reverberated earth, and distill it in a strong fire. Cohobate it four times, and so you shall have a very clear water which you must keep by itself. Then pour the air on the same earth, and distill it in a strong fire. There will come over a clear, splendid, odoriferous water which must be kept apart. After this pour the fire upon the first water, and putrefy them together in balneum the space of three days. Then put them into a retort and distill them in sand, and there will come over a water tasting of the fire. Let this water be distilled in balneum. What distills off, keep by itself, as also what remains in the bottom which is the fire, and keep by itself. This last distilled water pour again upon its earth, and let them be macerated together in balneum for the space of three days. Then let all the water be distilled in sand, and let what will arise be separated in balneum, and the residence remaining in the bottom be reserved with the former residence. Let the water be again poured upon the earth, be abstracted and separated as before until nothing remains in the bottom which is not separated in balneum. This being done, let the water which was last separated be mixed with the residue of its fire, and be macerated in balneum three or four days, and all be distilled in balneum that can ascend with that heat. Let what remains be distilled in ashes from the fire, and what shall be elevated is aerial. And what remains in the bottom is fiery. These two last liquors are ascribed to the two first principles, the former to mercury and the latter to sulphur. They are accounted by Paracelsus not as elements but their vital parts being, as it were, the natural spirits and soul which are in them by nature. Now, both are to be rectified and reflected into their center with a circular motion, so that this mercury may be prepared with its water being kept clear and odoriferous in the upper place, but the sulphur by itself.

Now, it remains that we look into the third principle. Let the reverberated earth, being ground upon a marble, imbibe its own water which did above remain after the last separation of the liquors made in balneum, so that this be the fourth part of the weight of its earth and be congealed by the heat of ashes into its earth. Let this be done so often, the proportion being observed, until the earth has drunk up all its water. And lastly, let this earth be sublimed into a white powder, as white as snow, the feces being cast away. This earth, being sublimed and freed from its obscurity, is the true chaos of the elements, for it contains those things occult, seeing it is the salt of nature in which they lie hid being, as it were, reflexed in their center. This is the third principle of Paracelsus, and the salt, which is the matrix, in which the two former sperms, viz., of the man and woman, the parents of the homunculus, viz., of mercury and sulphur are to be put, and to be closed up together in a glazed womb sealed with Hermes' seals for the true generation of the homunculus produced from the spagyrical embryo. And this is the homunculus or great arcanum, otherwise called the nutritive medicament of Paracelsus.

This homunculus or nutritive medicament is of such virtue that presently after it is taken into the body it is turned into blood and spirits. If then diseases prove mortal because they destroy the spirits, what mortal disease can withstand such a medicine that does so soon repair and so strongly fortify the spirits as this homunculus, being as the oil to the flame, into which it is immediately turned, thereby renewing the same. By this medicament, therefore, as diseases are overcome and expelled, so also youth is renewed and grey hairs prevented.

Lisiewski, in *Israel Regardie and the Philosopher's Stone*, attempts the work and is advised by Frater Albertus that the seeding ground or pre-adamite earth into which the sperm should be gestated is the universal Gur discussed at length in *The Golden Chain of Homer*.[1] 'First,' says Frater Albertus, 'we must do this little work of water, so you can acquire the keys to the animal kingdom of nature. Then you will be able to create the Homunculus.'

The Universal Gur of Nature is an incredibly important work, and one many alchemists spend years farming for their work.[2] An interesting account as to how to extract and perfect the Gur can be found in *The Golden Chain*; the most relevant sections we enclose for your examination:

THE UNIVERSAL GUR OF NATURE

Place this collected water (rainwater, snow, hail or dew) in a warm garret, where neither Sun nor Moon can shine upon it, cover the Vessels with a Linen Cloth, to prevent the dust getting into it.

Let it stand a month unmoved, and if the place is warm enough, you will by this time perceive an alteration in the water, because this water begins by the power of the implanted fire or spirit grow warm although imperceptibly and to break; it begins to ferment and putrefy and acquires a bad smell, and you will observe that it becomes turbid, although it was perfectly clear at first, and a brown spongy earth ascends swimming at the top, which increases daily and from its weight falls to the bottom.

Here you see a separation, occasioned by the ingrafted spirit of the gross from the subtil.

The separated earth is brown, spongy or like wool slimy and slippery, and this slimy earth is the Universal Gur of Nature.

Here the Artists may observe two things viz. water and earth, which conceal fire and air. Here the air animated by the fire is extended in the water. Now you have two passive Elements water and earth. In the beginning you had only a volatile water but by a gentle putrefaction in a warm place you have manifested the earth also. Fire and air we must look for in another way.

1 See *The Golden Chain of Homer* by Anton Josef Kirchweger.
2 For further details on this process see Jean Dubuis, *Philosophers of Nature*, details of which are given in our bibliography.

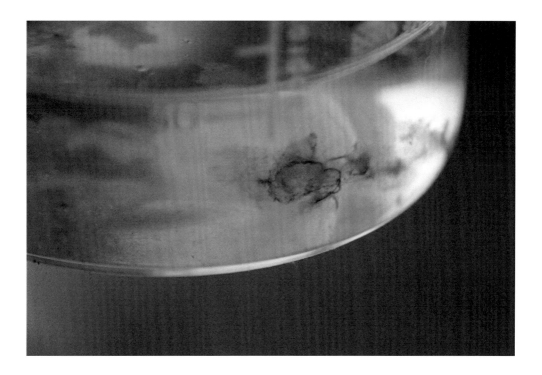

When you see now your Rain water in that state of putrefaction that the slimy Earth is separated and falls to the bottom. then stir it up with a clean wooden handle.

The Gur of Nature.
This is our Earth.

SEPARATION & DISTILLATION

Now pour your troubled water and earth in that state of putrefaction into a large Glass Body, which place in an earthenware pot, fixed into a charcoal distilling furnace, apply a large alembic and receiver and light your fire, which keep so gentle that only the stream or vapours arise. Let this all come over first as a pure water, which contains animated air, that is air and fire. Distil no more of the very volatile water over; than what will go with the gentlest degree of Heat, whilst the Subject in the body only vapours away but must not be suffered to boil, in this manner you vapour over about the fourth part of the whole, or less.

Take the receiver off with this very volatile water, this water the more so, if you afterwards rectify it *per se* over a steam bath is more luminous and clearer than common distilled water, which is a proof that it contains much air and fire.

Now apply another receiver and continue the distillation, raising your heat sufficiently, so as to cause the thickish water in the Glass Body to boil and in this manner you must distil all the water over, which will appear like water and in drops in the Alembic; continue the distillation until it remains in the body like melted Honey and looks Brown, but beware of distilling until it remains dry, because you would burn the young and tender Virgin earth in the bottom of the Vessel, which is not yet fixt. Take the distilled water away and put it by as the Element water.

The Honey-like Matter, or the moist earth remaining in the Glass body, take out cleanly and put it into a china basin and set it in the Sun to evaporate until it is perfectly dry; then grind it in a Glass Mortar to a subtil earth. Now you have separated the Elements out of your Chaos.

Now it remains to be proved that they are truly Elements or else it must be false what I have written, that all sublunary subjects proceed from them. To produce heavenly subjects out of this Chaos, or meteors, as this water itself is a meteorical production, let no one undertake; but we will demonstrate that Animals, Vegetables and Minerals may, and can be generated, and that is what we pretend and no further.

TO GENERATE MINERALS

Take your dried earth, put it into a glass Body and humect it a little with a few drops of your Dist: water, but not with the Element air and fire, and put the Body in a warm room facing the South, but let not the Sun's Rays shine upon the Body; after your earth is dry, humect or imbibe it again with the Element water. Then set it to dry, and this humecting and drying you may repeat several times every day and continue so doing during the whole Summer, and you can mineralise the whole Earth. You will find by your inbibitions and exsiccations, that the Earth becomes more ponderous and sandy.

N.B. the Glass Body must be covered with paper only to keep the dust out, as there must be left access of air. As soon as you perceive that the earth is become sandy, you may know that it is mineralised, this sandy earth is neither Animal nor Vegetable, consequently Mineral. If you have a few ounces of this earth, try it as Glauber tries the sun containing Sands and you will find a grain or two of sun and moon.

TO PRODUCE VEGETABLES OUT OF YOUR EARTH

Take your before mentioned earth dried in the Sun. put it into a Glass Body, make a mixture of two parts of water and one part of air (which you rectified in the beginning) with this humect or unbibe your earth as the gardeners do, by sprinkling only, not too wet, not too dry, place your Body (open) on the air not so that the Sun can shine upon it, and you will find several Vegetables productions spring up in a few weeks, although you have sown no Seed.

If you like to produce Animals. Take your before mentioned dried and powdered earth, pour first together, one part of water, and three parts of air, with this mixture humect your earth so copiously that it may become like liquid or melted Honey, place the Glass body which contains this mixture in the Air where it is warm, the Sun may shine on it but not too hot, nor at the Meridian, and the Glass is left open.

You will perceive that in a few days, there will be different kinds of small vermine, in the thick water; when the earth diminishes and dries up you must humect it again, so that it may remain of the same consistence like Honey or Syrup, as before; and you will perceive that the first small vermine will die and loose themselves, and others will be produced who will feed on their putrefaction and become larger and more in number.

I could reveal here something, but as it would be abused by profligate men, I am obliged to be silent.

You may be convinced by these experiments that our water or regenerated Chaos, Rain water, or Dew, or Snow is, and contains the Mundi and Universal Sperm, out of which, all things were, and are generated. It appears from this that this water and Earth are endowed with the principle of fertility for the three departments of Nature, as all things are produced thereof. Few there are that know the secret powers of these things, and what it is that causes and gives fertility!

It is a spirit or fire, but as a volatile unembodied spirit, he can effect nothing in natural productions.

Separating the pure from the impure

To ensure success Frater Albertus warns Lisiewski to be aware of air contamination and the need for 'electrified' water (gathered from a thunderstorm), as well as preventing contamination from entering into the apparatus, all being prerequisites for success.[1]

Finally, when this has been considered, the alchemist must feed the growing foetus, named, by Paracelsus, the arcanum of blood. The following recipe has been transcribed from Paracelsus's *Concerning the Nature of Things*:

> Let the blood be separated from its phlegm, which moves of itself, and is driven to the surface. Draw off this water by a dexterous inclination of the

1 Lisiewski charged his water.

vessel and add to the blood a sufficient quantity of the water of salt, which we teach you in our *Chirurgia Magna* how to make. This water at once mingles with the blood, and so conserves the blood that it never putrefies or grows rancid, but remains fresh and exceedingly red after many years, just as well as on the first day; which, indeed, is a great marvel. But if you do not know how to prepare this water, or have none at hand, pour on a sufficient quantity of the best and most excellent balsam, which produces the same effect. Now this blood is the Balsam of Balsams, and is called the Arcanum of Blood. It is of such great and wonderful virtue as would be incredible were we to mention it. Therefore you will keep this occult, as a great secret in medicine.

We are told by Lisiewski that Albertus warns him of the most common pitfalls: 'It will not be easy,' he cautions, 'you will most likely suffer several false starts until you get the hang of it; particularly with properly supplying the growing foetus with the Arcanum of blood and air. For the rate at which the blood flow is regulated is crucial, as is the fact that the blood must come from you – and from no one else. You are the father and must extend yourself into the mechanical procedures of nurturing by controlling the rate of blood flow to the foetus, just as the Gur will nurture by doing "her" part, constantly throughout the gestation period. Controlling the air flow will not be difficult as you will see. But controlling the blood flow, Ah! There's the rub!'

Practically speaking one must prepare an air pump, but by no means can contamination be allowed to enter the set up. Lisiewski suggests an air lock used in the fermenting of herbs, but the inner tube needs to be protected with Potassium bisulfite to maintain sterility.

Four grams of prepared gur was impregnated with sperm and by day 10 Liesiewski had nourished the grey mass with two feedings of arcanum of blood. 'Frater was right,' he records in his diary. 'The grayish mass absorbs the Arcanum at such a rate I could hardly believe my eyes.'

By day 30 during an aeration he notices a very sweet perfume exuding from the apparatus and a change in the mass, 'using a bright light and magnifying glass, I saw what appeared to be tiny red lines in the gur.' By day 45 we can almost feel his excitement: 'There is no question about it. The tiny red lines have become larger to me, they look like capillaries.' He increases the feedings to

170 ml of arcanum of blood and by day 60 he estimates it has grown by 30% to the size of a pea, the blood capillaries are clearer, whilst he maintains the same dose every five days and aerating the system every four days. By day 120 we are told that there appear 'two tiny appendage-like projections near the centre of the mass, and at the ends of them, what looks to be even tinier small humps or bumps.' Unfortunately by day 180 problems begin to occur, and although we can sense the alchemist doing everything he can to save his creation, by day 220 the creature is dead and we sense Lisiewski's loss as he emotionally confides: 'The experiment has ended. The thing died two days ago. I have not been able to face this failure, especially when I consider how much I gave to it in terms of everything that was required... As strange as it is to write this, I felt and still do feel a great emotional attachment to the little thing, and cried when I realised it died.'

With these words we end our inquiry into the mystery of homunculi.

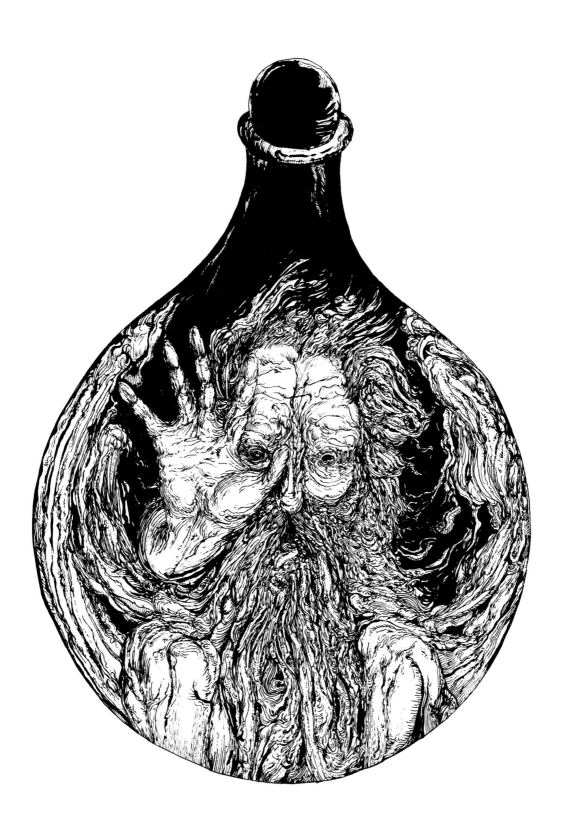

III

THE PHILOSOPHERS'
GARDEN

And first her fern-seed doth bestow
The kernel of the miseletow,
And here and there as Puck should go,
    With terror to affright him.
The nightshade straws to work him ill,
There with vervain and her dill
That hindereth witches of their will,
    Of purpose to dispight him.

Then sprinkled she the juice of rue,
That groweth underneath the yew,
With nine drops of the midnight dew
    From lunary distilling.

from Drayton's *Nymphidia*

The Gathering

The Norse people of old would use runes and charms to guide the gathering of herbs, the Eastern people also gathered herbs and prepared ointments using prayers and benedictions. We hear whispers of incantations and rituals being used to gather plants in Scandinavian myths, fragments of which would later migrate to British shores. But these are rare, partly due to men like Theodore, Archbishop of Canterbury, the attributed author of the *Penitential of Theodore*, who imposed strict penalties on any person practicing the old ways of gathering worts.

Some examples do survive, and we find in *The Leech Book of Bald*, a tenth century manuscript of Saxon origin, the following:

Against every evil rune lay,[1] and one full of elvish tricks, write for the be-witched man this writing in Greek letters: alfa, omega, IESVM,[2] BERON-IKH.[3] Again, another dust or powder and drink against a rune lay; take a bramble apple and lupins, and pulegium, pound them, then sift them, put them in a pouch, lay them under the altar, sing nine masses over them, put the dust into milk, drip thrice some holy water upon them, administer this to drink at three hours...

As Christianity's authority grew in Britain the monks, transcribing the early

[1] A runic charm.
[2] ΙΧΘΥΣ
[3] Which is to say the invocation of the image of Christ found on St. Veronica's kerchief.

herbals, replaced these heathen incantations and practices with biblical passages and prayers. The following example dates back to the fourteenth century, (although it is thought to be older), it runs thus:

> *Haile be thou holie hearbe*
> *Growing on the ground*
> *All in the mount Calvarie*
> *First wert thou found.*
> *Thou art good for manie a sore*
> *And healest manie a wound*
> *In the name of Sweete Jesus*
> *I take thee from the ground.*

The following incantation, gathered from Agnes Sampson,[1] a witch burned in 1590 (O. S.), is a 'Prayer and Incantation for visiting of sick folks.' It is entirely Christian and suggests the following formula should be incanted:

> *All kindis of illis that ewir may be, In Chrystis name, I coniure ye,*
> *I coniure ye, baith maire and les, With al the vertewis of the mess,*
> *And rycht sa, be the naillis sa, That naillit Jesus, and na ma;*
> *And rycht sa, be the samin blude, That reikit owre the ruithfull rwid;*
> *Furth of the flesch and of the bane, And in the eird and in the stane,*
> I CONIURE YE, IN GODIS NAME.

Among the most important rites and observations, as to when herbs were gathered, was when they were strongly influenced by their governing planet. Herbs under the dominion of the Sun were picked with either gold or stag horn, the stag's antler tines being symbolic of the sun's rays. In later herbals, and in the grimoire tradition, a white handled knife (the handle made of bone) is often used to gather herbs; the blade being made from copper, as this is said to prevent the plant from being 'determined' by steel or iron. For this reason purists would

---

1 It was said, at the trial of Elspeth Reoch 12 March 1616 that she was 'supernaturally instructed' to gather herbs by resting her right knee on the ground whilst pulling the herb 'betuix the midfinger and thombe, and saying of *In nomine Patris, Filii et Spiritus Sancti.*' See Dalyell, *The Darker Superstitions of Scotland Illustrated from History and Practice*, Waugh & Innes, Edinburgh 1834.

prefer to use a simple mortar and pestle instead of a food blender, but when dealing with kilograms of plant material this can become be a wearisome task. On this point I will defer to the sage advice of my friend and alchemical teacher, old Father Nottingham, whose reply, when I asked such questions, was always: *My dear boy, you must do as your Art demands!*

As physic changed from the four humours of Hippocratic medicine to the doctrine of signatures, the principle of sympathetic relationships between the body and the universe around us grew stronger. This helped physicians predict and control diseases by matching the sickness to the cure by means of the plant's *signatum*:

> The *Signatum* (or signature) is a certain organic vital activity, giving to each natural object (in contradistinction to artificially made objects) a certain similarity with a certain condition produced by disease, and through which health may be restored in specific diseases in the diseased part. This Signatum is often expressed even in the exterior form of things, and by observing that form we may learn something in regard to their interior qualities, even without using our interior sight.[2]

Plants, according to the doctrine of signatures, under Mars are of a 'hot,' temperament,[3] for example, black pepper and nettles. Bright yellow flowers are dedicated to the Sun, whereas pale yellow or white flowers are said to be under the watch of our Lady the Moon. These, both being luminaries, are said to be good for the eyes. Jupiter tends smooth leafed herbs, which may be slightly serrated and narrow, the veins on the underside of the leaves being neither ridged nor prominent. Herbs of Venus are those adorned with flowers of bright and delicate colours and pleasant odours. Mercurial herbs are said to be refreshing and more aromatic than others, whilst Saturn has dominion over gloomy green herbs, whose leaves are, according to Folkard, 'hairy, dry, hard, parched, coarse.'[4]

Since the days of the Druids, certain herbs have been gathered with the rising and the setting of the heavenly spheres, some being picked at the equinoxes,

2 See Hartmann, 1896: 'Cosmology,' p. 55.

3 Diseases were said to be formed by planetary signatures as is expressed in the four humours: red (Mars), black (Saturn), Yellow (Sun), white (Luna), to which the ancients accorded a sanguine, melancholic, choleric and phlegmatic temperaments respectively.

4 See Folkard's *Plant Lore, Legend and Lyrics*, Folkard & Son, London 1884.

whilst others at the eclipses of the sun and moon; or on the appearance of comets and at certain planetary conjunctions. To the Druids no journey was taken, no crops were sown, no timber felled and no hair was cut unless the moon was favourable to the undertaking. Indeed, a conjunction of a group of stars with a fixed body was considered the precursor for contagious disorders, whereas comets or shooting stars denoted putrefaction. Kircher, the famous Jesuit, went further when he declared that all putrid diseases prevailed according to where Mars and Saturn were placed. Dr Richard Mead (1673 – 1754) notes Kerckring's own extraordinary experience regarding a gentlewoman 'whose beauty depended on the lunar force, insomuch that at full moon she was very handsome, but in the decrease of the moon became so wan and ill-favoured that she was ashamed to go abroad.'[1]

According to Richard Mead: 'That birth and deaths chiefly happen about the new and full moon, is an axiom even among women. The husband-men likewise are regulated by the moon in planting and managing trees, and several other of their occupations. So great is the empire of the moon over the terraqueous globe.'

Many alchemists prefer to gather on the planetary day and hour of the herb, but it has been argued that, since changing to our modern calendar, the dates and days of the ancient pagan tradition have become problematic to ascertain. Calculating the planetary hours can assuage the purists, but in order to perfect the art of gathering, an astrological chart is considered the finest guide.

We hear Culpeper suggesting the time when herbs should be gathered: 'Fortify the body with herbs of the nature of the Lord of the Ascendant, 'tis no matter whether he be a Fortune or Infortune in the case. If the Lord of the Tenth be strong, make use of his medicines. If this cannot well be, make use of the medicines of the Light of Time.' The following chapter, Star Gathering, contains further suggestions.

In some Herbals specific days are chosen for the gathering, most commonly during the early days of May or St. John's Eve: 'All herbs pulled on May Day Eve have a sacred healing power, if pulled in the name of the Holy Trinity; but if in the name of Satan, they work evil.'[2]

In my experience, and once again I will be scowled at by purists, the most important aspect of the gathering *is* the gathering. And therefore my only advice

1   See Black, 1883.
2   See Wilde, *Ancient Legends, Mystic Charms and Superstitions of Ireland*, Ticknor & Co., 1887.

How could such sweet and wholesome hours
Be reckon'd but with herbs and flow'rs![4]

would be to step out of your front door, with your herb bag and staff, and go
a roving through the woods and the fields to discover for yourself what friends
and allies you might have among the wild grasses and weeds. Follow the moon
tides and gather the plants before they flower,[3] never too many from the same
spot, and always with reverence. Plants gathered before the sun rise are best,
since all their virtues are in them; during the day they work and by sunset are
exhausted and have less efficacy. Dry (assuming you're not proceeding with a
wet distillation of the plant, in which case freshly picked is best) in a dark, airy
space and when thoroughly dried, place them in an airtight container away from
direct sunlight. Most herbs will last a year, but after that they will lose their

3 It's worth noting those who wish to grow from seed should sow with the waxing of the moon and
   cut with the waning of the moon. Some Alchemists, as we shall see, prefer to use the seed alone.
4 Andrew Marvell, 'The Garden'

potency. When working with them, be of a cheerful heart and know that even though you have killed this little herb, you are resurrecting it and allowing it to fulfil the potential for which it has been created.

In terms of the part of the herb to be gathered, each plant is different and research is essential, but since each of the elements abounds in different parts of the herb, the entire plant is to be used in spagyrical preparations. If in doubt let us defer to those sage words of Gary Nottingham: *you must do as your Art demands!* Some alchemists prefer using the seed alone and on this point Glauber offers his worthy advice:

> If thou hast not so much Seed, thou may'st make the Medicine out of the whole Plant, as the Root, Stalk, Flowers, and Leaves: And the reason why I mentioned only Seed, was this, because the chief virtue of all the Vegetables, is occultly placed and concentrated in the Seed, else the whole Plant may (as aforesaid) be made use of, which although it yield not so much Oil as the Seed does, yet may we even this way receive a good quantity.[1]

Our herbarium is a compound of old wives' tales, herb lore, research and the snippets of forgotten wisdom gathered from living on the Shropshire borders. This knowledge is by its very nature a work in progress, and in no way to be taken as the final word on the subject of herbalism. To this end I have tried to include the time of their gathering, their planetary signature and finally their application. Each of us is tasked to create our own living herbarium from the plants we encounter and work with. When prepared by an alchemist, their power will be unlocked a hundredfold.

---

1 Glauber, Johann Rudolph (translated by Chris Packe), *A Spagyrical Pharmacopoeia*, Vol. I to VII, RAMS Digital

Star Gathering

The one became two by the law of polarity which is revealed within the three Essentials that will be found with the four Elements, wherein is to be found the Quintessence which is not of the Four, but one of the Three.   – ALCHEMICAL AXIOM

We have found the following correspondences useful and therefore include them for your reference:

MERCURY Plants under Mercury, gathered during the ascendance of Gemini or Virgo and while Mercury is in conjunction with the Moon, are used in diseases of the lungs.

JUPITER Plants under Jupiter must be gathered when Pisces or Sagittarius is ascendant, and Jupiter in conjunction with the moon, to cure the liver.

VENUS Plants under Venus must be gathered when the Moon is in Libra and in conjunction with Venus; they cure the kidneys.

SATURN Plants under Saturn are gathered when the Moon is in Capricorn and in conjunction with Saturn; they heal the spleen.

MOON Plants under the moon must be gathered when the Moon rises in Cancer and is conjoined with Jupiter; they heal diseases of the brain.

SUN Solar herbs should be gathered when the Moon rises in Sagittarius conjoined with Venus and Jupiter; they heal heart diseases.

Thou tellest my wanderings: put thou my tears into thy bottle: are they not in thy book? – PSALM 56:8

Consummation

The Lord hath created medicines out of the Earth; and he that is wise will not abhor them.
– ECCLESIASTICUS 38:4.

We now wish to speak about the consummation of our alchemical products. As we have said, birthed correctly these are highly actuated frequencies which having been transmuted, transmute. Once the seven products have been created some practitioners determine their elixirs with a drop of their own blood, gold solution or their own tears.

This locks the power of the tincture to the alchemist by building a sympathetic relationship between the vibrational frequency of the elixir and the field within the artist. These then are worthy of initiation as well as practical healing. Determined preparations, using blood or tears, cannot be shared with anyone else and are specific to the alchemist. To maintain their charge we place these elixirs on their relevant planetary kamea, either drawn on virgin paper or cast using their planetary metal, according to art. If in doubt, Gentle Philosopher, do as I did, and defer to those wise words of old Father Nottingham, and do as your art demands.

Tinctures of the Sun have positive effects and will raise our confidence, help us understand our position in the centre of the cosmos and fortify our energy centres. 'For those,' says Jean Dubuis, 'with a mystical inclination, the Sun can give and awaken consciousness to divine aims within the solar system and to divine will within the manifestation. The Sun also provides ambition, courage, dignity and authority.'

Alchemically prepared products will affect our unconscious mind and etheric energies. According to Dubuis, the Moon 'helps to realise the desires of those who are involved in psychic or initiatory research through hypnosis or self-hypnosis. This action on the subconscious enables one to drop a few destructive habits. For those interested in the research of past lives, it allows the consciousness to secure mastery of space and time. The Alchemist can thus obtain a clear vision of his past experiences and understand the reason for some of his actions that the present world cannot explain. If the lunar elixirs are properly charged and impregnated they can rapidly decrease the force of karma and even altogether eliminate all its negative effects. These elixirs are an important help for astral projection, because the Moon is the ruler of this domain and can unveil for you the forms, the functions and the rules of the astral.' He goes on to say, 'It modifies the aura in such a way that we can endure crowds better and our magnetic action on a crowd can be sensed better.'

Jupiter is the sphere of health and healing and will awaken our sense of justice and fair play, as well as developing our intuitive facilities to a greater degree. Dubuis relates, 'Jupiter is favourable to health, wealth and spirituality. If the elixirs are alchemically charged, the alchemist can penetrate the sphere of the lawfulness of the macrocosm and become capable of understanding the principles of the Tetragrammaton, the true name of Jupiter.'

Tinctures of Mars, says he, reinforce the function of the animal soul of man in all aspects and will develop all the elements necessary for the fight of survival and the instinct of self preservation. 'Mars,' he notes, 'can develop passions as well as reinforce muscle tone … the mystical expression of Mars is knowledge of space and time as a consequence of the action of the Pentagram. On a physical level, Mars favours telekinesis.'

Venusian products will develop the attractive centres of the soul, for Venus is Love, and Love is the means by which two opposites can be reconciled. She represents the law of attraction and, according to Dubuis, 'Venus increases the imagination as a result of a better sensitivity to astral influences which it provides. It makes relationships with others easier and gives a sort of inner harmony because of its balancing effect in the vibrations of the aura.' He goes on to say that if the products of Venus are properly charged they will open up the plant realm and, therefore, alchemists should take particular note.

Mercury acts on the intellect, quickening resourcefulness and reason. Mercury is the sphere of the imagination and is the binding principle between that which is above and that which is below.

Saturnian preparations will reinforce the physical body and help develop idealism in us, as well as patience and resolve. Saturn contains all and will give us the endurance and strength and foundation to assimilate the other tinctures.

Should we wish to mix our elixirs, Dubuis gives the following advice:

Mars has the distinction of reinforcing the action of all the others without modifying their orientation. The combination of Saturn with any other elixir reinforces the action on the terrestrial level.

A mix of elixirs of the Sun and Jupiter gives access to the highest level of evolution and thus provides a profound view of the philosophical principles and their roles in the cosmic sphere. The alchemist can also be in contact with his Masters of the past, receive their teaching and be able to teach in turn. On the material plane this combination fights depression by provoking cheerfulness.

A combination of Mars and the Sun is a powerful tonic at once mental and physical.

The combination of the elixirs of Mercury and Mars reinforces Mercury's effects and facilitates the manifestation of psychic powers (telekinesis for instance).

The combination of the elixirs of Mercury and the Moon increases the capacity of receptivity on the psychic and telepathic levels.

The combination Saturn/Mercury can directly lead to occult knowledge which is hidden because the Mercury of Saturn contains, through a karmic path, all the knowledge of Nature. For the same reason, the Philosophical Mercury extracted from Saturn opens the metallic Alchemical Temple.

We can also combine three elixirs, for example:

Saturn + Mercury + Moon yields revelation on plant alchemy
Saturn + Mercury + Sun provides revelation on metallic alchemy

Personally, I take five to ten drops of each elixir three times a day, (Moon tinctures on Monday et cetera). These products have an accumulative effect and one should not be surprised to notice an increase of vitality, well being and intuition.

The Herbarium

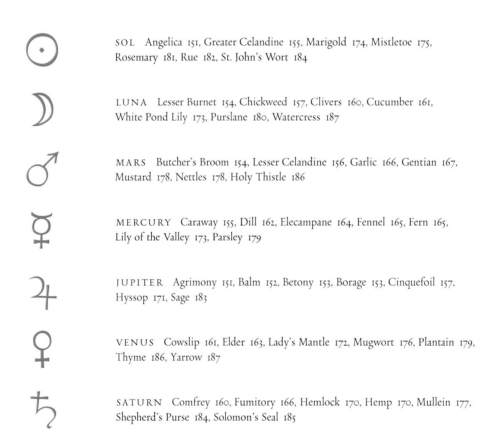

AGRIMONY

Gerard says it is 'good for them that have naughty livers.' It was once a favourite of herbalists who were said to be able to heal gout, sore throats, ague, colic, ear-ache, cancer and ulcers with it. According to Culpeper it removes disease due to its sympathy to Jupiter, healing and strengthening those parts under its planet and sign, as well as healing those that fall under Saturn, Mars and Mercury by antipathy.

'This herb,' adds Culpeper, 'also helps the cholic, cleanses the breast and rids away the cough…it is a most admirable remedy for such whose livers are annoyed either by heat or cold. The liver is the former of blood, and blood the nourisher of the body, and Agrimony a strengthener of the liver.'

Agrimony makes an excellent spagyrical tincture.

NAME
Agrimonia eupatoria
DOMINION
Jupiter hath dominion
PARTS USED
Root and herb

ANGELICA

It was said to have been given to mankind by the Angel Gabriel and was considered a cure-all, as well as offering sovereign protection in cases of witchcraft and sorcery. The Laplanders were wont to crown their poets with it as it was said to inspire them. According to Gerard, the root hung about the neck will ward off witchcraft.

Mrs. Grieve says: 'The root, stalks, leaves and fruit possess carminative, stimulant, diaphoretic, stomachic, tonic and expectorant properties, which are strongest in the fruit, though the whole plant has the same virtues.'

Angelica is excellent in driving away stubborn colds and has been used in pulmonary cases to great effect. To make an infusion, pour boiling water over the root, reduce, add fresh water, reduce again and when ready bottle. Two table-spoons three or four times a day are considered to be effectual in the above cases.

Culpeper says: 'the decoction drank before the fit of an ague, that they may sweat (if possible) before the fit comes, will, in two or three times taking, rid it quite away.'

NAME
*Angelica archangelica,
Root of the Holy Ghost*
DOMINION
The Sun rules
ARTS USED
Seeds, root and leaves

NAME
Melissa officinalis
DOMINION
*Jupiter calls her his own.
Paracelsus says it is a herb under
the government of the Sun*
PARTS USED
Leaves and flowers

As we've seen, Paracelsus believed Balm to revivify the human body and regenerate it. Indeed, in the *London Dispensary* of 1696 we find a similar view: 'an essence of balm, given in Canary wine, every morning will renew youth, strengthen the brain, relieve languishing nature and prevent baldness.' Hartmann goes so far as to praise Balm as a source of concentrated quintessence, equal to blood.[1]

Folkard[2] gives an account of the legend of the Wandering Jew, who met the Nazarene carrying the cross to Golgotha, who sinking exhaustedly to his knees asked the Jew Ahasuerus for a cup of water. Ahasuerus spurned his request and bade him on his way, to which Jesus replied: *I go, but thou shalt thirst and tarry till I come.* From that moment forth Ahasuerus was doomed to wander the earth, thirsting for water and waiting the hour of judgement, until one day having walked for centuries he knocked on the door of an old Staffordshire cottager to beg refreshment. Though the cottager was gravely ill and dying of consumption, he received him and gave him beer and when Ahasuerus had finished his cup he asked the man what ailed him. After which Ahasuerus said: *Friend, I will tell thee what thou shalt do and by the help and power of Almighty God above, thou shalt be well. Tomorrow, when thou risest up, go into thy garden, and gather there three balm leaves and put them into a cup of thy small beer. Drink as often as you need, and when the cup is empty, fill it again, and put in fresh balm-leaves every fourth day, and thou shalt see, through our Lord's great goodness and mercy, that before twelve days be past, thy disease shall be cured and thy body altered.* Declining to eat, Ahasuerus left and was never seen again, but the cottager did as the stranger suggested and 'before twelve days were passed was a new man.'

As a means of strengthening the memory and driving away melancholy this fragrant little plant has been held as a sovereign remedy. According to Gerard it gives much profit if planted next to bee hives. He observed the bees rubbing themselves against the leaves which 'causeth others to come unto them.' Pliny also noted the curious affinity the bee has to this singular herb; a few leaves placed in a hive will make it agreeable to the swarm.

As we have seen, an Ens of this herb has reputedly miraculous properties.

1 Hartmann, 1896, p. 300.
2 Folkard, *Plant Lore, Legends, and Lyrics*.

BETONY

Antonius Musa, the physician of the Emperor Augustus, is traditionally considered the author of a treatise on Betony showing it cured no less than 47 diseases.

It is a nervine and used for headaches, sharp pains in the head, neuralgia and hysteria. Gerard attests: 'It preserveth the lives and bodies of men from the danger of epidemical diseases. It helpeth those that loathe and cannot digest their food.'

Turner, in his *British Physician* of 1687, tells of this famous herb: 'It would seem a miracle to tell what experience I have had of it. This herb is hot and dry, almost to the second degree, a plant of Jupiter in Aries, and is appropriated to the head and eyes for the infirmities whereof it is excellent, as also for the breast and the lungs; being boiled in milk, and drunk, it takes away pains in the head and eyes.'

NAME
Betonica officinalis, Stachys betonica, Stachys officinalis, Bishops wort
DOMINION
Jupiter
PARTS USED
Herb and roots; dry thoroughly and store in tight containers

BORAGE

In 1810 Dr. Thornton called it 'one of the four grand cardiac plants.' It has long been a herb of joy, driving away melancholy and comforting the heart. It was considered to be a member of the so called 'cordial flowers' used since classical times to cheer the spirits, the other three being Roses, Violets and Alkanets. According to Gerard, the leaves used in salad will 'exhilarate and make the mind glade.' The leaves and flowers steeped in white wine will make those who take it merry, whilst a decoction or tea will calm excitable or nervous dispositions.

It was due to its joyful nature that it was remembered in the old verse: *ego borago, gaudia semper ago.**

Bees love this herb and a fine honey can be made from the flowers. Alchemists will be interested to note that the leaves are loaded with nitre. To test this throw some dried leaves on the fire!

NAME
Borago officinalis, Euphrosinum
DOMINION
Jupiter
PARTS USED
The leaves before blossoming & to a lesser degree the flowers

* *I Borage, bring alwaies courage.*

BURNET, LESSER

No ear hath heard, no tongue can tell,
The virtues of the pimpernel[1]

NAME
Pimpinella saxifraga,
Burnet Saxifrage
DOMINION
The moon owns this herb *
PARTS USED
Herb and root

**There is confusion as to the*
government of this herb. Culpeper,
whose advice has been followed thus
far, says that the Greater Burnet,
Sanguisorba officinalis, is considered
a solar herb; whilst the lesser,
Pimpinella saxifraga, with which we
are concerned, is a lunar herb. Other
authors have claimed that the lesser
is also under the Sun. We have
maintained Culpeper's stance
on the matter.

Traditionally, the sword of the magus ought to be steeped in mole's blood and the juice of this herb. In Piedmont, Pimpinella was common currency between the womenfolk, as it was said to increase their beauty.

Mrs. Grieve says that the lesser, with which we are concerned, is a capital wound herb, in that it is styptic and an infusion of the whole herb being employed as an astringent was held in much repute. 'Turner,' says she, 'advised the use of the herb, infused in wine or beer, for the cure of gout and rheumatism.' Culpeper says 'some women use the distilled water to take away freckles or spots in the skin or face; and to drink the same sweetened with sugar for all the purposes aforesaid.'

We read in *The Folk-lore of Plants*[2] that in Hungary this noble herb has a long and mystic history and is popularly nicknamed Chaba's salve, 'there being an old tradition that it was discovered by King Chaba, who cured the wounds of fifteen thousand of his men after a bloody battle fought against his brother.'

BUTCHER'S BROOM

NAME
Ruscus aculeatus,
Knee Holly, Sweet Broom
DOMINION
Mars rules this herb
PARTS USED
Herb and root:
the shoots should be gathered
in Spring, the root in Autumn

Culpeper says, of this noble plant of Mars: 'the decoction of the root made with wine opens obstructions, provokes urine, helps expel gravel and the stone, the stranguary and women's courses, also the yellow jaundice and the head-ache; and with some honey or sugar put thereunto, cleanses the breast of phlegm and the chest of such clammy humours gathered therein.'

Mrs. Grieve says that in cases of jaundice or the gravel: 'one pint of boiling water to 1 ounce of the twigs or ½ ounce of the bruised fresh root has also been recommended as an infusion. In scrofulous tumours, advantage has been realised by administering the root in doses of a drachm every morning.'

1 Anon.
2 Thiselton-Dyer, T.F., 1889.

CARAWAY

There is a strange myth that the seeds deposited in or on any object would prevent it from being stolen. For this reason many love potions used Caraway to bind a lover. Interestingly, it has been noted that pigeons, given baked caraway bread, will never stray the coop.

Mrs. Grieve tells us that: 'both fruit and oil possess aromatic, stimulant and carminative properties. The bruised seeds pounded with the crumb of a hot new loaf and a little spirit to moisten, was an old fashioned remedy for bad earache. The powder of the seeds, made into a poultice, will also take away bruises.'

Four drops on a lump of sugar is said to be good for flatulence; the distilled water is said to be an excellent remedy for infants troubled with colic.

Jean Dubuis makes a plant stone using Caraway which he says initiates the user to the sphere of Hod (Mercury).

NAME
Carum carvi
DOMINION
Mercury hath lordship of this herb
PARTS USED
Whole herb

CELANDINE, GREATER

It was called Chelidony from the Greek *chelidon* (swallow), as it was said to flower with their coming and fade at their departure.

Although this herb has built a reputation for its medicinal properties, Paracelsus hints at more occult virtues: 'For who shall teach us,' notes our guide, 'that we may know by what powers the quintessence of antimony throws off the old hair and makes new hair grow; why the quintessence of balm destroys the teeth, eradicates the nails of the hands and the feet, and restores new ones; the quintessence of rebis strips off and renews the skin; and the quintessence of celandine changes the body and renovates it for the better, as colours renovate a picture?'

Arthur Edward Waite writes: 'Paracelsus calls chelidonia a constelled remedy, and names it as a powerful specific for certain ulcers which he also calls constelled. There was, moreover, a philosophic salt of chelidonia, which was medically applied by the alchemists. The same herb was regarded as a preventive of plague, and it was used as a remedy for jaundice. The plant is better known as swallowort or celandine. Chelidonia is also said to be a secret name of gold.'

NAME
Chelidonium majus,
Common Celandine
DOMINION
It is of a solar nature
PARTS USED
Herb and root

Culpeper says it should be gathered when the sun is in Leo for it is a solar plant and for this reason, he says that the eyes benefit well from this noble herb. 'For if this does not absolutely take away the film, it will so facilitate the work, that it might be done without danger.'

Mrs. Grieve informs us that its medicinal properties have been used as a purgative and diuretic, while being highly prized in cases of eczema and other 'scrofulous diseases,' suggesting an 'infusion of 1 ounce of the dried herb to a pint of boiling water being taken in wineglassful doses. The infusion is a cordial and greatly promotes perspiration. The addition of a few aniseeds,' she continues, 'in making a decoction of the herb in wine has been held to increase its efficacy in removing obstructions of the liver and gall.'

It is said that the strongly pungent juice is good for sharpening the sight, as well as for curing warts, ringworm and corns, having being applied directly. In which case pour one pint of boiling spring water on one handful of green tops. We have made a magistery of this herb and it served us well.

CELANDINE, LESSER

NAME
Ranunculus ficaria,
Pilewort, Figwort
DOMINION
Mars hath dominion
PARTS USED
Herb and roots

Due to its signatum, small grapelike appendages at the roots, this cheerful little herb has been long used for piles, interestingly enough this is a singular remedy. Externally immerse the herb in warm lard or clarified butter, simmer, strain repeat and then finally pour into pots. Cool before applying! Culpeper says this ointment is excellent in removing hard knots, 'kernels' and tumours found about the neck and ears.

For sore throats, this old time remedy was much used:

Take a pinte of whitewine, a good handful of sallendine, and boil them well together; put it in a piece of the best Roach Allome, sweeten it with English honey and use it.

Alternatively, infuse 1oz of the herb in a pint of water and take in wineglass doses.

CHICKWEED

Chickens love this little herb and there is no place on the planet that it does not grow. Gerard counts at least thirteen species and Mrs. Grieve notes that the flowers open roughly at 9 am and stay open for 12 hours. She gives it as 'an instance of what is termed the "Sleep of Plants," for every night the leaves approach each other, so that their upper surfaces fold over the tender buds of the new shoots, and the uppermost pair but one of the leaves at the end of the stalk are furnished with longer leafstalks than the others, so that they can close upon the terminating pair and protect the tip of the shoot.'

Used mainly as an ointment it was boiled in hog's fat to make a fine cooling ointment, which Mrs. Grieve notes is 'good for piles and sores and cutaneous diseases.'

A decoction of the herb is said to be good for constipation. Chickweed tea is an old remedy for obesity.

NAME
Stellaria media,
Starweed, Passerina
DOMINION
The Moon owns this little herb
PARTS USED
Herb

CINQUEFOIL

A recipe for witches' ointment in Mrs. Grieve's *Modern Herbal* runs thus: 'The juice of five-leaf grass, smallage and wolfsbane is mixed with the fat of children dug up from their graves and added to fine wheat flour.' We suspect it is a recipe for a flying salve. Note that wolfsbane is highly toxic and we cannot recommend its use even if, by using hemp oil as a base, or lard, rather than child fat, a modern day rendition of this recipe could be achieved. Cinquefoil was also used in the green language of heraldry, the five leaves denoting Man's five senses. Only those few men and women who had mastered their senses had the right to wear cinquefoil.

It was also used in love divination. Find a cinquefoil, which has seven leaflets, and put it under your pillow. 'You will then dream of your lover, and the person about whom you dream "you surely will have, as sure as the dead man lies in his grave."'[1]

NAME
Potentilla reptans,
Five leaf grass, Five-fingers
DOMINION
Jupiter hath dominion
PARTS USED
Root and herb

---

1 Friend, *Flowers and Flower Lore.*

Mugwort

Feverfew

Greater Celandine

Clivers

Plantain

Valerian

Elecampane

Fennel

NAME
*Galium aparine,
Cleavers, Goose Grass*
DOMINION
The Moon owns this herb
PARTS USED
*Seed and herb,
not so much the root*

This humble and well recognised herb has a huge range of properties making it a truly marvelous plant. Well known as a diuretic, tonic and alterative. Goosegrass cleanses the blood like no other plant and therefore is widely used in chronic cases of scurvy, scrofula diseases and psoriasis.

A wash made of the plant eases sunburn and removes blemishes and freckles on the skin, especially if applied with a cloth to the face and neck; whereas Culpeper notes, if boiled in hog's grease (lard or clarified butter are to be used) it is said to remove tough knots and swellings around the throat.

The herb bruised and applied will ease sores and blisters and as Mrs. Grieve attests: 'The herb has a special curative reputation with reference to cancerous growths and allied tumours, an ointment being made from the leaves and stems wherewith to dress the ulcerated parts, the expressed juice at the same time being used internally.'

Lady Northcote confirms its anti-tumour properties: 'Cliders (goosegrass, Galium aparine) was much given for tumours and cancers, and is praised by other than merely village sages.'

In Dr. Thornton's *Herbal* of 1810, we read: 'After some eminent surgeons had failed, he ordered the juice of Cleavers, mixed with linseed, to be applied to the breast, in cases of supposed cancer of that part, with a teaspoonful of the juice to be taken every night and morning whilst fasting, by which plan, after a short time, he dispersed very frightful tumours in the breast.'

Preparing an Ens of clivers is a worthy alchemical exercise.

COMFREY

NAME
*Symphytum officinale,
Yalluc (Saxon), Knit Bone*
DOMINION
Saturn hath dominion
PARTS USED
Roots and leaves

Famed for its ability to heal bruised and broken bones, it was grown in medieval gardens as a universal wound heal. Its botanical name is derived from the Greek *sympho* (to unite) and the common name is a corruption from the Latin *con firma*, alluding to this noble herb's ability to mend bones.

A spagyrical tincture would be best made from the root of the herb, but a decoction or tea of the root taken every three hours is said to be a marvelous remedy for piles and internal bleeding, whether from the lungs, stomach or bowels. Applied externally, the leaves have a reputation for treating sprains, swellings and gangrenous sores. We find more than one author suggesting that a hot poultice applied to the gout will offer immediate relief.

COWSLIP

Gerard says decoction of the leaves and flowers are an excellent remedy for gout and 'slacknesse of the sinews, which is the palsie.' He also suggests a decoction of the roots, which he says is profitable to the stone in the kidneys and bladder. Pope writes:

> — if your point be rest,
> Lettuce and cowslip wine: probatum est.

NAME
Primula veris,
Fairy Cups, Petty Mullein
DOMINION
Venus lays claim to
this gentle herb
PARTS USED
Flowers and leaves

Cowslips were once taken as nerve and brain strengthener and were excellent for insomniacs prepared as a wine.

Taken regularly it stops the shakes and is a great remedy for illnesses issuing from the head, including, attests Culpeper: 'false apparitions, phrensies, falling sickness, palsies, convulsions, cramps.'

'Some weomen,' according to Turner, 'sprinkle ye floures of cowslip wt whyte wine and after still it and wash their faces wt that water to drive wrinkles away and to make them fayre in the eyes of the worlde rather then in the eyes of God, Whom they are not afrayd to offend.'

Culpeper also attests to their cosmetic virtues. 'Our city dames know well enough the ointment or distilled water of it adds to beauty or at least restores it when it is lost.' Cowslip is now, alas, an endangered species; use very sparingly.

CUCUMBER

The seeds ground and rubbed with water created an emulsion which was held to be an excellent cure for catarrhal affections and diseases of the bowels. It is of high cosmetic repute, a slice rubbed over the skin will keep it soft and supple, cooling and soothing skin irritations. A recipe for Cucumber lotion follows thus:

NAME
Cucumis sativus, Cowcumber
DOMINION
This fruit owes its allegiance
to the Moon
PARTS USED
Whole fruit

Peel 1 or 2 large cucumbers, slice and place in the upper part of a steamer. When soft place in a muslin bag and squeeze out all the juice. Add to this one-fourth of rectified spirit of wine and one third elderflower water. Stir or shake the mix and pour into bottles for use.

A recipe for Cucumber perfume can also be given:

Peel 9lbs of cucumber and cover with spirit of wine. Place in an incubator and leave for a few days. Separate the alcohol and squeeze the juices from the cucumber in a muslin bag and pour both over fresh cucumbers and return to the incubator. Express the liquid filter and bottle for use.

Culpeper says: 'Take the cucumbers and bruise them well, and distil the water from them, and let such as are troubled with ulcers in the bladder drink no other drink. The face being washed with the same water, cures the reddest face that is; it is also excellently good for sun-burning, freckles and morphew.'

DILL

NAME
*Peucedanum graveolens,
Anethon, Fructus Anethi*
DOMINION
It is of a mercurial nature
PARTS USED
*Harvest the seeds either early
morning or early evening; the
lower first, the higher can dry
on the stalks. Once gathered
dry in the sun*

Derived from the Norse word, *dilla*, to lull, on account that the seeds were given to babies to make them sleep. *The Leech Book of Bald* suggests, for head ache, take blossoms of dill, seethe in oil, smear the temples therewith.

It is an herb under Mercury and therefore interesting to note it was much used by witches and wizards for their work, especially in binding potions and love philters. In Drayton's *Nymphidia* we hear the following:

> *She night-shade strawes to work him ill,*
> *Therewith her vervayne and her dill*

Chiefly carminative, a spagyrical tincture of the seed provides stomachic, stimulant and aromatic properties. Up to five drops of the distilled oil on a lump of sugar has been used in the past to alleviate trapped wind, and it was considered a household essential, especially as a children's medicine. In addition the oil has been used for perfuming cosmetics and soaps.

ELDER

Although this sacred tree is technically not an herb, this Herbarium would be incomplete without mention of this ancient guardian. The Hylde-moer (Elder-mother) or Hylde-qvinde (Elder-woman) will watch both your hearth and herbs, for both are under her protection. Women in Sweden who are pregnant readily kiss the tree to gift them a safe and easy birth.

The Danes believed anyone fool enough to use elder as furniture or to board their floors with it would be doomed to a life of misfortune and if a child should be laid in a cradle fashioned from her wood, the Elder Mother will pull the child from it while it slept.

To share her gifts, one must petition her with sweet words. The following supplication was delightfully told to me by a farmer's wife whilst out walking:

> Elder Ma, Elder Ma, gi' me a' finger ta mak me whol,
> And I'll give me thine, when I lie in ma hole.*

Another supplication runs more simply, and is one I use when necessity calls: *Elder Mother, Elder Mother allow me to take thy branches.* If no objection is made, the gatherer should take what they need and spit three times at the roots of the tree to seal the pact.

An example of how disease can be transplanted into an Elder goes thus: 'For three nights running take three spoonfuls of bathwater in which an invalid has been bathed and pour them under an Elder saying: *Elder Mother, Elder Mother, the Lord hath sent me, that thou may take my sickness upon thee.* As a means of transplanting Ague, a twig may be gathered, after the above petitions are made, and stuck into the ground, you then leave, without speaking or looking back. The disease will then pass into the twig and attach itself to the first person who approaches the spot.

In France they do things differently; if livestock have been tormented or contaminated by vermin, they lead the animal to the foot of an Elder-tree, and twirling a bough in their hands, they bow to the tree, and address her, saying: *Madam, if thou doth not rid me of this tribe of vermin I shall be forced to cut off your limbs.*

NAME
Sambucus nigra,
Black Elder, Pipe Tree,
Hylder, Hylantree (Saxon)
DOMINION
Her lady Venus rules her
PARTS USED
Bark, flowers, leaves and fruit

* Note how similar this is to a formula which I noted from an old herbal:

Lady Elder, give me some of thy wood, and then will I also give thee some of mine when it grows in the forest.

In Denmark it is said that the spirit of the Elder Mother is kindly to humans, driving away evil spirits that 'do affright them' and give long life and bounty to those who ask graciously. It is said that he who stands under her boughs 'at twelve o'clock on Midsummer Eve, will see Toly, the king of the elves, go by with all his train.'

Franz Bardon recommends using an elder wand picked from hallowed ground, packed with ground amber and plugged at the end.

To wash away a maiden's freckles, Sir Hugh Platt in his *Delights for Ladies* of 1659, gives this recipe: 'Wash your face, in the wane of the Moone, with a sponge, morning and evening, with the distilled water of Elder-leaves, letting the same dry into the skinne. Your water must be distilled in May. This from a traveller who hath cured himself thereby.'

Along the borders here, wise folk still bury their sins and sorrows under the Elder.

ELECAMPANE

NAME
Inula Helenium,
Elf Dock, Horse Heal
DOMINION
The noble Mercury rules her
PARTS USED
Flowers and Roots. Gather the
flowers in June or July, the roots
in autumn. Gather from plants
at least 2 years old.

So named (legend has it) after the nosegay carried by Helen when Paris stole her away to Troy. The Romans grew the herb for its root, which they cooked and ate like a vegetable. Christian monks grew it for making the heart glad and for easing chest and lung conditions.

Gerard says that it is good for shortness of breath and its ability to ease asthma. When sucked, the candied root is said to help remove 'tough and clammy humours, which sticke to the chest and lungs.'

The root, gently boiled and then chewed, is also said to strengthen loose teeth.

More recently a report from a research student at Cork University of Technology, Ireland, showed that extracts from the herb kills MRSA bacteria and a broad spectrum of other bacteria.

FENNEL

In ancient times fennel and St. John's wort were used to prevent and protect against witchcraft. Many herbalists, from Pliny up to modern times, have noted that this herb is a strength giving plant, particularly for the sight. The seeds, bruised and covered in water, were once used as a calmative, and an elixir will strengthen the constitution. At one time fennel was a very popular restorative and it was said to convey longevity. Longfellow wrote these lines on it:

> Above the lowly plant it towers,
> The fennel, with its yellow flowers;
> And in an earlier age than ours
> Was gifted with the wondrous powers
> Lost vision to restore.
>
> It gave new strength and fearless mood,
> And gladiators, fierce and rude,
> Mingled it in their daily food,
> And he who battled and subdued,
> The wreath of fennel wore.

NAME
Fœniculum vulgare,
Fenkel, Sweet Fennel
DOMINION
Mercury owns this herb
PARTS USED
Seeds, leaves and roots

FERN

Much magick is tied to this well known plant. Its power to render the owner of its elusive seeds invisible was common currency once upon a time and many sought, upon the eve of St. John, its sacred seeds. Gadshill writes: 'We have the receipt of fern-seed, we walk invisible.'

In Grimm's *Teutonic Mythology* we read how: 'a man in Westphalia was looking on midsummer night for a foal he had lost and happened to pass through a meadow just as the fern seed was ripening, so that it fell into his shoes. In the morning he went home, walked into the sitting-room and sat down, but thought it strange that neither his wife nor any of the family took the least notice of him. "I have not found the foal," said he. Thereupon everybody in the room started and looked alarmed, for they heard his voice, but saw him not. His wife called

NAME
Pteris
DOMINION
Mercury hath dominion over
this magical herb
PARTS USED
The seed should be gathered
midnight at the Eve of St. John

him, thinking he must have hid himself, but he only replied, "Why do you call me? Here I am right before you." At last he became aware that he was invisible, and remembering how he had walked in the meadow on the preceding evening, it struck him that he might possibly have fern-seed in his shoes. So he took them off, and as he shook them the fern-seed dropped out, and he was no longer invisible.'

A receipt for gathering the seed can be found in a manuscript dating back to Queen Elizabeth's reign: 'Gather fearne-seed on Midsomer Eve, and weare it about the continually…gather the fernseed on Midsomer Eve betweene 11 and 12 at noone and at night' Some say the seeds should be gathered by placing silver plates under the ferns, but by no means should one shake or force the seeds into falling.

FUMITORY

NAME
*Fumaria officinalis,
Earth Smoke, Beggary*
DOMINION
Saturn is lord over this herb
PARTS USED
Whole herb

Legend has it that this herb was born from the vapours of the earth and interestingly it is rarely pollinated by insects, but self-fertilises. In ancient times magicians used the herb in their exorcisms, the smoke being noxious to spirits.

Mrs. Grieve says it should be used as a 'weak tonic, slightly diaphoretic, diuretic and aperient; valuable in all visceral obstructions, particularly those of the liver.'

In respect of skin ailments much has been said about this slender and delicate little plant, and Dr Cullen rather dramatically warns us that, if the 'empire of beauty be in jeopardy,' due to 'neglecting the parasol,' the infusion of the leaves is an 'excellent specific for removing these freckles,' best used by those who have 'previously removed those moral blemishes which deform the mind, or degrade the dignity of a reasonable and an immortal being.' In other words, freckles.

GARLIC

NAME
Allium sativum
DOMINION
Warlike Mars rules this herb
PARTS USED
Bulb

The ancient Greeks would place garlic cloves, piled at the crossroads, to appease Hecate, goddess of the Moon. Were a man to chew a piece of garlic whilst running he would apparently prevent his competitors getting the better of him. The same is said of jockeys, who would fasten garlic to the bits of their horses to prevent the other riders pulling ahead, the horses being offended by the smell. Mrs.

Grieve notes that Mountstuart Elphinstone says: 'The people in places where the Simoon (poisonous wind) is frequent eat Garlic and rub their lips and noses with it when they go out in the heat of the summer to prevent their suffering from the Simoon (heatstroke).'

Throughout the First World War garlic was commonly used as an antiseptic, the raw juice being diluted with water, placed on sphagnum moss (previously sterilised) and applied to the wound.

During an outbreak of infectious fever it was said that the French doctors, who ate garlic constantly, seemed to visit the worst cases with impunity. Mrs. Grieve says a syrup of garlic is an 'invaluable' cure for 'asthma, hoarseness, coughs, difficulty of breathing and most other disorders of the lungs.'

Garlic syrup is easy to prepare. Firstly bruise as many bulbs as you wish and cover with boiling water. When they are soft, separate, dry and keep aside. Then add a cup of distilled vinegar to the liquid before reducing. Next add a good dollop or two of honey. Reduce to a syrup on a gentle heat and then pour over the dried bulbs. A spoonful of this mixture should be taken every morning. This syrup is also said to be good for rheumatism, as well as dropsy (water retention), tubercular illnesses and epilepsy.

The quintessence of garlic would be a worthy alchemical project and one we would love to hear about should you, Gentle Philosopher, wish to take up the challenge.

GENTIAN

There are 180 species of *Gentiana* and all of them are famed for their bitter properties. Mrs. Grieve describes it as 'one of the most useful of our bitter vegetable tonics. It is specially useful in states of exhaustion from chronic disease and in all cases of general debility.'

The dried root, powdered, and taken in wine is said to open obstructions in the liver and restore appetite. Steeped in wine, Culpeper says it is refreshing and restorative, especially for those who 'be over weary with travelling, and grow lame in their joints…it is an excellent remedy for such as are bruised by falls.'

An excellent stomach tonic can be made thus: For a simple tincture prepare 2oz of gentian root, ½ oz of bruised cardamom and 1oz of dried orange peels in 1 litre of brandy.

NAME
*Gentiana,
Baldmoney, Felwort,
Bitterwort*
DOMINION
Mars rules this herb
PARTS USED
Root and herb

Hemlock

Watercress

Cowslip

Shepherd's Purse   *Yarrow*

Lady's Mantle   169

HEMLOCK

NAME
Conium maculatum.
Spotted Corobane.
Kex, Kecksies
DOMINION
Saturn rules this dread herb
PARTS USED
Herb, seeds and root

Folkard tells us that snakes flee from its leaves: 'It is the Coneion of the ancients: that deadly poison distilled from the juices of the Hemlock, that was drunk by Socrates, Theramenes, and Phocion – the fatal drug given to him whom the Areopagus had condemned to death – the unfailing potion gulped down by ancient philosophers, who were weary of their lives, and dreaded the infirmities of old age.'

Pathless, lost and resolved to their fate, these men crowned themselves with garlands of the leaves and flowers and with weak smiles upon their lips they took the fatal cup of Coneion.

In Russia it is considered a Satanic herb. In Germany it was used in funeral rituals. In England it was much used by witches in their 'hell-broths,' and in ancient Greece the Eleusinian priests would rub their bodies with it.

Outwardly we may use it to break tumours, swelling and pains in the joints as well as cancerous ulcers when it is made into a poultice or ointment, but on no account should one partake of the herb inwardly for fear of death.

HEMP

NAME
Cannabis sativa
DOMINION
Saturn rules this herb
PARTS USED
The dried flowers of the female

Even in Herodotus' time hemp was used recreationally and brought into Thrace from Scythia. We're told in *Plant Lore, Legends and Lyrics*: 'A curious prophecy relating to English kings and queens, and the prosperity of England, has been preserved by Lord Bacon, who heard of it when Queen Elizabeth was "in the flower of her age":

> *When Hempe is spun,*
> *England's done.'*

On account that rope was made from hemp, it has been used in love divination and binding rites. To bind a lover one should prepare hemp thread and 'twenty five needlefuls of coloured silk' and at midnight plait them, saying:

> *Chistu é cànnavu di Christu,*
> *Servi pi attaccari a chistu.*

Then go to church and at the moment of consecration of the host, tie three knots in the plait, into which one has added the persons hair. Having tied it, one should invoke the names of certain spirits to turn the loved one's affection towards oneself.

In modern times, such people as Rick Simpson have shown that cannabis can actively reduce a range of cancers. Although the following receipt is not an alchemical preparation, we enclose Simpson's instructions for making cannabis oil, and although we cannot condone the use of illegal substances, the weight of evidence to support his claim makes it worth noting. At the time of writing, legalisation proceeds apace.

Gather 4 oz of cannabis and place it a freezer. Place 2 litres of isopropyl alcohol in the freezer. Next day place the cannabis in a funnel and pour the alcohol over the herb. Collect the yellowish liquid and repeat three times with fresh alcohol, each time washing the herb with the alcohol instead of steeping it. Filter through coffee filters and place over a gentle water bath to evaporate the alcohol until you are left with a thick oil. To make sure you have removed all the isopropyl alcohol out of the oil, add a few tea spoons of distilled or spring water and 'wash' the oil gently, gently stirring all the time. When ready, store in glass jars and consume by dipping a finger into the oil on a regular basis.

HYSSOP

Throughout history this has been considered a sacred plant used in the purification of temples and consecrated spaces. From the Old Testament onwards, we see hyssop being used for ritual washes, as noted in the Psalms of David. In Exodus 12:21-22, we read Moses ordering the Children of Israel:

> Draw out and take you a lamb according to your families, and kill the Passover. And ye shall take a bunch of hyssop, and dip it in the blood that is in the bason, and strike the lintel and the two side posts with the blood that is in the bason; and none of you shall go out of the door of his house until the morning.

Moses directed them to do this so that the Lord could identify the Israelites from the Egyptians:

NAME
Hyssopus officinalis
DOMINION
Jupiter rules this herb
PARTS USED
Flowering tops

...and when he seeth the blood upon the lintel and on the two side posts, the Lord will pass over the door, and will not suffer the destroyer to come in unto your houses to smite you.

Hyssop was also one of the herbs used in the aspergillum of Solomon, although there has been much argument as to whether the hyssop referred to in the Bible is actually *Hyssopus officinalis*. Some authors have suggested that the scriptures refer to common marjoram, others say it is in fact *Capparis spinosa*, which the Arabs call *azaf* or holy herb.

The flowering tops, covered in boiling water and made into a tea three times a day, are said to be an excellent remedy for rheumatism, but a spagyrically prepared tincture would have, according to Mrs. Grieve, the following medicinal value: 'Expectorant, diaphoretic, stimulant, pectoral and carminative.'

An infusion of ½ tablespoon of dried hyssop flowers, covered in a pint of boiling spring water for ten minutes and sweetened with honey and lemon, taken by the wineglass has been used for centuries for pulmonary complaints, especially to ease asthma.

LADY'S MANTLE

NAME
Alchemilla vulgaris.
Lion's foot
DOMINION
Venus call this herb her own
PARTS USED
Herb and root

Lady's mantle is famed for restoring vitality and according to Hoffman, it has the power of 'restoring feminine beauty, however faded, to its early freshness.'

It has been held in high repute as preserving long life, and one highly recommends creating an Ens of this gentle plant. The name *Alchemilla* refers to the dew that collects in abundance on its leaves, which is subsequently used in alchemical preparations.

Mrs. Grieve confirms, along with many authors, that its leaves have been used to treat inflamed wounds, and that it was formerly considered one of the best wound herbs.

A decoction of the dried herb taken by the wine glass relieves menstruation. Some old authors suggest a sprig of the fresh leaves under the pillow will promote a quiet sleep.

LILY OF THE VALLEY

This sweet flower's name, Magalis or Majalis intimates *that which belongs to May*; for this reason Culpeper says that it is a Mercurial herb, for in the Greek myths, Maia, the daughter of Atlas, was the mother of Hermes, the winged messenger of the gods.

To capture the sweet smell of the flowers, immerse them (fresh) in either almond oil or olive oil, strain and repeat until the oil is perfectly saturated.

It is used mainly as a cardiac tonic, which, according to Mrs. Grieve, slows the disturbed action of a weak, irritable heart, whilst at the same time increasing its strength. It is also said to ease nicotine poisoning.

Culpeper commends it for weak memories, loss of speech, apoplexy and gout. The distilled water from the fresh herb is said to be a sure cure for nervous affections and dropsy caused by an irregular heart. For this reason it was kept in containers made of gold or silver.

Gerard recommends the following method of extracting its precious golden liquor: 'The floures of May Lillies put into a glasse, and set in a hill of ants, close stopped for the space of a moneth, and then taken out, therein you shall finde a liquor that appeaseth the paine and griefe of the gout, being outwardly applied.'

NAME
Convallaria magalis.
May Lily. Our Lady's Tears
DOMINION
It belongs to the House
of Mercury
PARTS USED
The herb, root and flowers

LILY, WHITE POND

Mrs. Grieve says that the root contains 'tannin, gallic acid and mucilage, starch, gum, resin, sugar, ammonia, tartaric acid, fecula, etc.' The roots can also be applied topically, as a poultice and have done good service in the 'healing of boils, tumours, scrofulous ulcers and inflamed skin.' Mrs. Grieve adds 'a complete cure of uterine cancer by a decoction and a vaginal injection is recorded.' Usage is as follows: infuse an ounce of root in a pint of water for 30-45 minutes, strain and take in teacup doses three times a day.

Culpeper writes: 'An ointment made of the root, and hog's grease, is excellently good for scald heads, unites the sinews when they are cut, and cleanses ulcers…the ointment is excellently good for swellings in the privities, and will cure burning and scaldings without a scar, and trimly deck a blank place with hair.'

NAME
Nymphaea odorata
DOMINION
The moon hath dominion
over this beautiful plant
PARTS USED
The fresh root gathered during
the wane of the moon

MARIGOLD

NAME
Calendula officinalis
DOMINION
The Sun owns this herb
PARTS USED
Flowers and leaves

In his meditations, written at Carisbrooke Castle, Charles I rather mournfully records:

> *The Marigold observes the Sun,*
> *More than my subjects me have done.*

The myth that the marigold follows the sun is of ancient origin and Shakespeare makes mention of this a number of times, particularly in *Cymbeline*, and *The Winter's Tale*:

> *The marigold, that goes to bed wi' the sun*
> *And with him rises weeping.*

We are warned to gather this herb only when 'the moon is in the sign of the virgin' and not when Jupiter is in the ascendant, as the virtues of this noble plant would be much diminished. The parts used are the flowers and leaves, which are best gathered in the morning when the dew has been dried by the first rays of the sun. This herb is very much a solar plant and is fabled to lift the spirits and strengthen the heart.

'This herb,' says Culpeper, is 'of the sun and under Leo... The flowers, either green or dried, are much used in possets, broths, and drink, as a comforter of the heart and spirits.'

It is both a stimulant and a diaphoretic and, blended into a pap and applied as a poultice, has been known to soothe varicose veins. The expressed juice of the plant has been recommended as a natural wart remover in some parts of the country. An old superstition says that one would only need to look upon this sacred little flower for all evil humours to be drawn from the head and the sight to be strengthened.

Marigold tea has been widely administered in the past as a remedy for measles, but perhaps the most curious of receipts comes from Albertus Magnus who says, in his *Book of Secrets*: 'The vertue of this herbe is mervelous, for if it be gathered, the sunne beynge in the sygne Leo, in August, and be wrapped in the leafe of a Laurell, or baye tree, and a wolves tothe be added therto, no man shalbe able to have a word to speake agaynst the bearer thereof, but woordes of peace.'

A recipe for toothache suggests steeping marigolds in vinegar and rubbing the gums with the resulting liquid.

I made an alchemically prepared tincture from the flowers and have been much impressed by how this little plant lifts up the spirits and warms the heart. A few drops added to a bottle of mineral water and sipped throughout the day exhilarates the soul.

MISTLETOE

It is a herb ruled by the Sun, yet Culpeper suggests that, when it grows on an oak tree, for example, it would 'participate something of the nature of Jupiter.'

In Shakespeare's *Titus Andronicus* we hear the lines:

> *The trees, though summer, yet forlorn and lean,*
> *O'ercome with moss and baleful mistletoe;*

A reference to the myth of Baldr the beautiful, the Apollo of the Scandinavian myths, best beloved son of Odin the Wanderer.

Legend says that on dreaming of the death of Baldr, his mother Frigg made every stone, flower and animal swear an oath not to hurt her child. All made the oath except, that is, a small sprig of mistletoe. The apple tree on which the plant grew had readily agreed, but Frigg failed to make the oath with this herb. Since nothing could kill Baldr, the gods amused themselves by throwing weapons and objects at the him, all of which failed to hurt him. In the midst of the celebrations Loki took a branch of mistletoe which he'd fashioned into an arrow and placed it in the bow of the blind god, Höðr, Baldr's brother. The shot, fired by Höðr, guided by Loki, hit Baldr, slaying him. In an account given by Mrs. Grieve, Baldr 'was restored to life at the request of the other gods and goddesses, and mistletoe was afterwards given into the keeping of the goddess of Love, and it was ordained that everyone who passed under it should receive a kiss, to show that the branch had become an emblem of love, and not of hate.'

According to Mrs. Grieve, mistletoe excels as a nervine and antispasmodic and has a 'great reputation for curing the "falling sickness" (epilepsy) and other convulsive disorders (Agues in the old tongue).' Indeed, Sir John Colbatch hailed its virtues in a pamphlet called *The Treatment of Epilepsy by Mistletoe*.

NAME
Viscum album
DOMINION
His Majesty the Sun
rules this herb
PARTS USED
The young leaves and shoots,
gathered before the berries grow
and when the moon is
six days old

Dried and hung around the neck it is said to ward off witchcraft and according to Culpeper: 'Both the leaves and berries of Misselto do heat and dry, and are of subtle parts; the birdlime doth mollify hard knots, tumours, and imposthumes; ripens and discusses them, and draws forth thick as well as thin humours from the remote parts of the body, digesting and separating them.'

The dried leaves and young shoots can be powdered or it can infused or tinctured spagyrically or alternatively immersed in white wine. A decoction can be made by boiling 2oz with half a pint of water, a tablespoon being taken a few times a day.

MUGWORT

NAME
*Artemesia vulgaris,
Herb of St. John the Baptist,
Maiden's wort & sometimes
Motherwort; in Russia it is called
Zabytko, the herb of forgetfulness*
DOMINION
It gives its allegiance to Venus
PARTS USED
The young shoots and flowers

The mugwort is addressed as 'Una' (First), the 'eldest of worts' in the Old English 'Nine Herbs Charm.' In the *Herbarium* of Pseudo-Apuleius it is written: 'And if a root of this wort be hung over the door of any house then may not any man damage the house.' In the *Leech Book of Bald*, we find:

For mickle travelling over land, lest he tire, let him take mugwort to him in hand, or put it into his shoe, lest he should weary, and when he will pluck it, before the upgoing of the sun, let him say first these words, 'I will take thee, Artemisia, lest I be weary on the way,' etc. Sign it with the sign of the cross, when thou pullest it up.

The Italian peasants used mugwort to tell if someone would recover from their illness. Without telling the patient, a sprig of the plant was placed under the pillow and if they slept, it meant they would recover. If they did not sleep, it meant they would die.

It has long been used by skryers for awakening the third eye prior to ritual and an elixir will enhance dream-working. Note this well.

Portions of the dead root can be found at the base of the plant and were once called 'coals,' being considered a preventative of epilepsy when taken internally or hung about the neck. Indeed, if taken regularly, its anti-epileptic properties will soon become evident, followed by profuse and fetid perspirations.

It is said to be useful against the gout, by boiling the fresh tops into a tea and drinking regularly.

MULLEIN

With unmistakable tall stalks, often adorned in yellow or white flowers, this plant can reach four or even five feet tall. Its leaves spread over the ground and are covered with a fibrous downy hair, it flowers in July or August. Gerard writes: 'Apuleius reporteth a tale of Ulysses, Mercurie, and the inchauntresse Circe, and their use of these herbes in their incantations and witchcrafts.' An ointment made of hog's grease (butter or lard being a natural substitute) and placed on piles is said by him to be a sovereign remedy. 'The leaves,' says he, 'worne under the feet day and night in manner of a shoo sole or sock, bring downe in yong maidens their desired sicknesse, being so kept under their feet that they fall not away.'

A decoction of the root is said to strengthen the stomach and a decoction of the flowers is said to ease stomach pains. Culpeper notes, 'The decoction of the root in red wine or water, (if there be an ague) wherein red hot steel hath been often quenched, doth stay the bloody-flux. The same also opens obstructions of the bladder and reins (kidneys).'

In Germany a wash is made from the herb, which is said to be a 'capital restorative of the hair.'

Culpeper also heralds this royal herb as being excellent for gout, three ounces of the distilled water made from the flowers being 'drank morning and evening for some days together.'

However, mullein is best known for its ability to soothe chest troubles and it is said that it was for this reason that the Romans brought it to England. A simple recipe for this would be to boil a handful of leaves, fresh or dry, in a pint of milk for ten minutes, strain and drink whilst warm twice a day. It is said that Dr. Quinlan of Dublin cured 'many cases of tubercular lung disease, even when some were far advanced in pulmonary consumption, with the Mullein, and with signal success as regards palliating the cough, staying the expectoration, and increasing the weight.'

NAME
Verbascum thapsus,
Hag's Taper
DOMINION
Old Saturn rules this herb
PARTS USED
Leaves and flowers

MUSTARD

NAME
Brassica nigra
DOMINION
Mars owns this mighty herb
PARTS USED
Seeds

Two oils can be retrieved, the first by expressing the seeds and the second by adding water and distilling. The water left over from a distillation can be used with great effect in the cleansing of the skin.

Medicinally, the oil taken inwardly and outwardly is said to promote hair growth. Culpeper says, 'the seed taken either by itself, or with other things, either in an electuary or drink, doth mightily stir up bodily lust and helps the spleen and pains in the sides and the gnawings in the bowels.'

A poultice of the fresh leaves can be used to reduce knots and swellings around the throat and, if applied to sciatica pains, gout, aching joints or any other part of the body, it will ease the pain and draw out the humours.

NETTLES

NAME
Urtica dioica, Greater Nettle &
Urtica urens, Lesser Nettle
DOMINION
Mars hath dominion
PARTS USED
The whole plant for spagyrical tinc-
tures, leaves and tops
for teas and food

Urtica, the name of the genus to which the various stinging nettles belong, is derived from the Latin *uro*, to burn, and the *Urtica pilulifera* variety was said to have been introduced by the Romans to keep themselves warm, which they did by rubbing their bodies all over with this fiery plant. In Scandinavian mythology nettles were sacred to Thor, and up until the thirties peasants would throw nettles onto their fires whenever there was a thunderstorm to appease the god, petitioning him not to strike their homes.

Paracelsus recommends nettles for all 'tartaric diseases' where too much sediment in the body is said to cause arthritis or sciatica. In medieval times peasants afflicted with arthritis thrashed the afflicted part with the herb, but an elixir is preferable.

During the trial of Katherine Oswald for witchcraft, it was stated that she had cured a boy of the 'trembling fever…by plucking up a nettle by the root, throwing it on the hie gate, and passing on the cross of it, and returning home, all which must be done before sun-rising;' she repeated this 'for three several mornings, which being done, he recovered.'[1]

---

1 Grant, *Old and New Edinburgh*.

PARSLEY

In Devonshire, it is said that to move parsley from its bed is to cause offence to its guardian spirit: if not appeased, the spirit will cause misfortune or death within the year, either to the offender or a member of their family. The Greeks held parsley in the uttermost respect, the victors of the Isthmian Games were adorned with dried garlands of the herb and at banquets they would wear garlands in their hair as they said it inspired quietness and promoted an appetite. It furthermore had strong funerary symbolism and was intimately connected with Persephone and the Eleusinian mysteries. For this reason it is considered a herb of misfortune. This idea is also found in south Hampshire, where in older days, the country folk would on no account give parsley to one another for fear that misfortune should befall them.

The volatile oil contains Apiol, which has proved excellent in cases of ague. Mrs. Grieve says, 'Parsley has carminative, tonic and aperient action, but is chiefly used for its diuretic properties, a strong decoction of the root being of great service in gravel, stone, congestion of the kidneys, dropsy and jaundice.

NAME
Carum petroselinum
DOMINION
Mercury owns this herb
PARTS USED
Root and seed

PLANTAIN

In folklore it is said the plantain was a beautiful maiden, who waited for her long lost love to return from the wars. Such was the length of her solitary vigil that she finally grew roots and turned into the Weybroed (or Weybrood), which accounts for why this gentle herb can still be found waiting by the hedgerow.

In the Anglo-Saxon *Lacnunga*, the plantain appears as 'the Mother of Herbs'in the 'Nine Herbs Charm' and is an ingredient of the remedy that accompanies 'Wið færstice,' the charm against sudden stitch, notable for its references to the Aesir and elves. In the United States it is known as Snake weed due to its reputation for healing poisonous bites, and in Scotland it is called Slan-Lus, *plant of healing*.

A decoction or tea of the root was said to be a noble remedy for disorders of the reins (kidneys) and the juice of the plant mixed with lemon juice was said to be an excellent diuretic.

NAME
Plantago major,
Waybroad, Slan-lus,
Cuckoo's bread, Ripple Grass
DOMINION
Venus loves her
PARTS USED
Roots, leaves and flowers

Salmon's Herbal, 1710, says that plantain was used in a fine cosmetic, added to houseleeks and lemon juice. Culpeper says it is under the command of our Lady Venus and is good for treating spreading skin diseases, such as shingles, scabies and ringworm. It was meant to be especially useful for mad dog bites, but is chiefly known to alleviate bee stings and the inflammation of the skin.

Shakespeare has this to say about it:

> ROMEO *Your plantain leaf is excellent for that.*
> BENVOLIO *For what, I pray thee?*
> ROMEO *For your broken shin.*

A Shropshire love charm runs thus: Take a leaf of plantain and place it in your mouth and incant:

> *Where the sun sees thee*
> *Shall my love be with me,*
> *Where the sun lies down,*
> *In his (her) arms I'll be found.*

The leaf is then cut finely and sprinkled in the lover's food.

PURSLANE

NAME
Portulaca sativa
DOMINION
The Moon hath power of this herb
PARTS USED
Whole herb, juice and seeds

Strewn about the circle of art it is said to ward off evil spirits, and strewn about a bed is said to bring happiness.

Fresh leaves applied to the eyes will allay swelling and the leaves can be eaten in salads. Culpeper says if the herb is held under the tongue it will assuage thirst and if 'applied to the gout, it eases pains thereof and helps the hardness of the sinews, if it come not of the cramp, or a cold cause.'

Mrs. Grieve notes its uses in cooling 'heat in the liver' and to ease pains in the head.

An alchemically prepared tincture will soothe inflamed gums and will also fasten loose teeth. The seeds bruised and simmered in wine, which after being strained, is bottled and given to children, a spoonful a time, is good for worms in the stomach.

John Heydon, in his *Holy Guide*, gives the following recipe to *beautifie the skin*: 'Take Wild Purslaine, Mallow, Nightshade, Plantain with the seeds, of each three handfuls. The Whites of 12 Eggs, Lemons number 12; Roch Allum, 4 ounces; prepare and diſtil them according to Art.'

ROSEMARY

According to Culpeper this is a solar herb, but because the heart and the head are in affinity with one another, the herb was renowned for being good for the memory and an emblem for fidelity. It was often entwined about the bride's wedding wreath, richly decorated in coloured silks. It was also one of the main funeral herbs, a sprig of which was often given to mourners as they left the house: they would then carry this to the church and throw it on the coffin as it was lowered. In *Romeo and Juliet*, Friar Laurence alludes to the practice by saying: *Dry up your tears and stick your Rosemary on this fair corse.*

The ancients used rosemary in incense for religious ceremonies and as a safeguard against witches' spells and the evil eye. In the 19th and early 20th century, French hospitals mixed it with juniper berries and burned the resultant incense to clear the air from pathogens; similarly sprigs of it were hung in sick chambers, and a sprig under a child's pillow is said to ward off bad dreams.

In the *Grete Herball* we find another use of rosemary as incense: 'Rosemary. For weyknesse of ye brayne. Agaynſt weyknesse of the brayne and coldenesse thereof, sethe rosmaria in wyne and lete the pacyent receye the smoke at his nose and kepe his heed warme.'

Whereas in Bancke's herbal we find the following advice: 'Take the flowers thereof and make powder thereof and binde it to thy right arme in a linnen cloath and it shale make thee light and merrie. Take the flowers and put them in thy cheſt among thy clothes or among thy bookes and mothes shall not deſtroy them. Boyle the leaves in white wine and washe thy face therewith and thy browes and thou shalt have a faire face.'

Used externally, as a hair tonic it was said to stimulate the follicles and prevent premature balding. A recipe for infusing the dried herb, both the leaves and flowers, in borax and leaving it to go cold was at one time considered to be one of the best hair washes available and over time promised to be a natural remedy for scurf and dandruff.

NAME
Rosmarinus officinalis,
Polar Plant, Compass-weed
DOMINION
The Sun hath dominion
PARTS USED
Roots and herb

RUE

He who sows hatred, shall gather rue.

NAME
*Ruta Graveolens,
Herb of Grace*
DOMINION
It is a solar herb
PARTS USED
*The entire herb, but the tops
of the young shoots are best*

*Danish proverb

Those who follow the left hand path will know this ancient plant. Spurned lovers take the shoe of their ex-partner and fill it with rue to cause harm. Yet it has also done good service over the ages in protecting against witchcraft, and was used by the Greeks for this purpose. Rue is an herb connected with repentance and it has been said that an aspergillum made of rue was used to purify the altar before High Mass. A magic wreath was woven by maidens from rue, willow and cranesbill, and 'walking backwards to a tree they throw the wreath over their heads, until it catches on the branches and is held fast. Each time they fail to fix the wreath means another year of single blessedness.'

The name comes from the word *ruta*, from the Greek, *reuo* (to set free), on account of this ancient herb's ability to relieve various diseases. Pliny the Elder celebrates rue's ability to preserve and sharpen the sight. Milton, who was totally blind by the time he composed these lines, tells of how:

> *Michael from Adam's eyes the filme remov'd
> ...then purged with euphrasie and rue
> the visual nerve.*

It said that the god Hermes gave Odysseus an antidote against the beverage of the enchantress Circe which contained rue. It is still used in Italy to ward off the evil eye.

Rue water was used to sprinkle a house infested with fleas, and the leaves, when chewed, will relieve nervous headaches, giddiness and panic attacks.

Be careful of this herb.

SAGE

Sage is a truly extraordinary herb. The botanist Hilderic Friend wrote of it as an example of a sympathetic relationship between plants and the people who tend the land: a Buckinghamshire farmer once informed him that it 'would thrive or decline as the master's business prospered or failed. He asserted that it was perfectly true, for at one time he was doing badly, and the sage began to wither; but as soon as the tide turned the plant began to thrive again.'

Salvia is from *salvo*, to save, due to its healing properties, but far beyond that, more than one author has noted this noble herb's ability to render men immortal. So says Evelyn: 'In short 'tis a Plant endu'd with so many and wonderful Properties, as that the assiduous use of it is said to render Men Immortal.'

According to an old French saying:

> *Sage helps the nerves and by its powerful might*
> *Palsy is cured and fever put to flight.*

The ancients used it for the embalming of bodies and interestingly Mrs. Grieve notes that the active principle 'confers the power of resisting putrefaction in animal substances.' Stimulant, astringent, tonic and carminative, sage is still used as a key ingredient in mouthwashes. As a tea it purifies the blood and eases fevers, Mrs. Grieve provides the following recipe: 'Half an ounce of fresh sage leaves. 1oz of sugar, the juice of 1 lemon infused in a quart of boiling water and strained after half an hour.'

Culpeper says, 'Sage is of excellent use to help the memory, warming and quickening the senses.' Although I haven't personally attempted making an Ens of this sacred plant, it is definitely on my wish list.

NAME
Salvia officinalis.
Garden Sage. Salvia salvatrix.
Sage the Saviour
DOMINION
Jupiter rules this herb
PARTS USED
The whole herb

The name of this herb's genus signals its occult nature: *hypericum* is derived from the Greek *hyper eikon*, meaning 'over an apparition,' denoting its use as a fumigatory to ward off evil spirits; because of these properties, Paracelsus was much enamored by this herb. 'The veins,' remarks our guide in *De Naturalibus*, 'upon its leaves are a signatum, and being perforated, they signify that this plant drives away all phantasmata existing in the sphere of man. The phantasmata produce spectra, in consequence of which a man may see and hear ghosts and spooks, and from these are induced diseases by which men are induced to kill themselves, or to fall into epilepsy, madness, insanity, &c. The hypericum is almost a universal medicine.'

A fine oil can be made by infusing the flowers in olive oil. It has an astringent nature and a reputation for curing chronic pulmonary conditions and easing bladder troubles. So much so, that a tea made from the leaves or flowers is said to stop children wetting the bed.

An old Gaelic incantation, uttered in the Hebrides (Carmichael, 1900) runs as follows:

> St. John's wort, St. John's wort,
> My envy whosoever has thee,
> I will pluck thee with my right hand,
> I will preserve thee with my left hand,
> Whoso findeth thee in the cattlefold,
> Shall ne'er be without kine.

SHEPHERD'S PURSE

Saturn nurses this herb, whose name derives from the small seed pods, which look like tiny purses. Culpeper says it helps fluxes of the blood, bloody urine and spitting of blood. Mrs. Grieve confirms this, saying many herbalists use this little plant to stop hemorrhages of the lungs, stomach, uterus, and especially the kidneys. Made into a poultice it offers a sovereign remedy for inflammations and bruises and the expressed juice of the plant being dropped into the ears is said by this experienced author to be good for tinnitus, or as the Master puts it: 'The juice being dropped into the ears, heals the pains, noise and mutterings thereof.' It has also been recognised as a fine means of resolving 'the grit and sand of the kidneys,' strengthening the urinary tract and relieving swelling of the spleen; it is also said to soothe liver complaints and jaundice. In some parts of the country it was used by sheep farmers to reduce cancerous tumours in their flocks and is said to have the same effect upon humans.

SOLOMON'S SEAL

Saturn is severe, indeed Binah heads the Pillar of Severity, and Solomon's seal is true to its signatum in that it is a strong binding herb and was often used to seal fresh wounds. A decoction, 1oz to a pint of water, is said to be very beneficial in cases of consumption and 'bleeding of the lungs.' It is a hardy, elegant plant, serenely beautiful, and possessed of a mixed personality, owing one part to its nature, the other to its character.

Its nature is, as we have said, Saturnine for it has been used to heal bones, bruises and inflammations either by its being laid upon the affected area or by the patient taking a decoction of the dried root in wine or water. In parts of Shropshire the flowers are still steeped in beer (though white wine is preferable), which is said to strengthen loose teeth.

The wise Gerard writes: 'That which might be written of this herbe as touching the knitting of bones, and that truely, would seem unto some incredible; but common experience teacheth, that in the world there is not to be found another herbe comparable to it for the purposes aforesaid.'

This herb has been used as an excellent cosmetic. As Culpeper says: 'The decoction of the root in wine ... or the distilled water of the whole plant, used to the face, or other parts of the skin, cleanses it from morphew, freckles, spots, or marks whatsoever, leaving the place fresh, fair, and lovely; for which purpose it is much used by the Italian Dames.'

NAME
Polygonatum multiflorum,
Lady's Seal, St. Mary's Seal
DOMINION
Old Saturn owns this herb
PARTS USED
Roots dug in Autumn

NAME
Carbenia benedicta
DOMINION
Mars rules this herb
PARTS USED
Herb

This has not been called the holy thistle without reason, for nearly all the ancient herbalists cherished this sacred herb. It is said to have great power in cleansing and purifying the blood. Mrs. Grieve quotes Matthiolus and Fuschius, who write: 'It is a plant of great virtue; it helpeth inwardly and outwardly; it strengthens all the principle members of the body, as the brain, the heart, the stomach and the liver, the lungs and the kidney; it is a preservative of all disease for it causes perspiration, by which the body is purged of much corruption, such as breedeth diseases; it expelleth the venom of infection; it consumes and wastes away all bad humours; therefore give God thanks for his goodness.'

We are told there are four ways in which we can take this herb. The first is to eat the leaves fresh in bread and butter, much like a salad herb; second, the leaves can be dried and then powdered and a drachm added to a glass of wine; thirdly, as a decoction of the dried herb; and the fourth way is to exalt it to its First Entity.

THYME

NAME
Thymus serpyllum,
Mother of Thyme,
Serpyllum
DOMINION
Venus loves this herb
PARTS USED
Whole herb

We speak of wild thyme which, like foxglove and wood sorrel, has long been a favourite of the faerie folk. In *A Midsummer Night's Dream* we hear of a magickal place:

> *I know a bank whereon the wild thyme blows*
> *Where ox-lips and the nodding violet grows;*
> *Quite over-canopied with lush woodbine,*
> *With sweet musk-roses and with eglantine.*

We give a receipt, dated 1600, for an oil, 'To enable one to see the Fairies': 'A pint of sallet oyle (olive oil) and put it into a vial glasse; and first wash it with rose-water and marygolde water; the flowers to be gathered towards the east. Wash it till the oyle becomes white, then put into the glasse, and then put thereto the budds of hollyhocke, the flowers of marygolde, the flowers or toppes of wild thyme, the buds of young hazle, and the thyme must be gathered neare the side of a hill where fairies use to be: and take the grasse of a fairy throne; then all these put into the oyle in the glasse and sette it to dissolve three dayes in the sunne and then keep it for the use.'

Garden thyme is the 'improved' form, cultivated from the wild plant. Both are 'an antiseptic, antispasmodic, tonic and carminative.' Culpeper says it is an excellent remedy for shortness of breath and in an ointment takes away 'hot swellings and warts.' It is a gallant enemy of gout and is said to take away the hardness and swelling of the spleen.

Gerard affirms its ability to heal sciatica and 'pains in the head,' but we are warned never to bring wild thyme into the home as it is said to bring death or severe illness along with it.

WATERCRESS

Be warned not to confuse it with the poisonous marshwort or 'Fool's cress.' Its Latin name is derived from *nasus tortus*, 'a convulsed nose,' due to its strong odour. Culpeper says 'they are more powerful against the scurvy, and to cleanse the blood and humours than Brooklime is, and serve all in all the other uses in which Brooklime is available, as to break the stone and provoke urine.'

The bruised leaves or juice is said to be an excellent skin cleanser, especially from spots, freckles and discolouration.

'The juice,' says Culpeper, 'mixed with vinegar, and the fore part of the head bathed therewith, is very good for those that are dull and drowsy, or have the lethargy.'

Mrs Grieve suggests a dosage of 1 to 2 fluid ounces of the expressed juice, and mentions that watercress 'has also been used as a specific in tuberculosis.'

NAME
Nasturtium officinale
DOMINION
The moon owns this herb
PARTS USED
Whole herb

YARROW

It has been named darkly: Devil's nettle, Bad man's plaything and Devil's plaything, due to being an ingredient in sorcery and magic. It has long been used in divination. According to Mrs. Grieve, in the eastern counties of England, 'there is a curious mode of divination with its serrated leaf, with which the inside of the nose is tickled while the following lines are spoken. If the operation causes the nose to bleed, it is a certain omen of success:

NAME
Achillea millefolium, Milfoil,
Yarroway, Devil's Nettle,
Soldier's Woundwort,
Knight's Milfoil.
DOMINION
Venus loves this herb
PARTS USED
Whole herb

Yarroway, Yarroway, bear a white blow,
If my love love me, my nose will bleed now.'

The following method to discover a vision of a future husband or wife was in vogue not so long ago: sew an ounce of the herb into a sachet and place it under the pillow before going to bed, having recited the following incantation :

Thou pretty herb of Venus's tree,
Thy true name is Yarrow;
Now who my bosom friend must be,
Pray tell me tomorrow.

Mrs. Grieve describes yarrow as diaphoretic, astringent, tonic and stimulant. It is a native of the British Isles. One of the best ways of taking this agreeable herb is by decoction or hot infusion before retiring to bed. Yarrow tea is excellent for stubborn colds and a decoction of the herb is said also to be good for piles. It has been used to treat rheumatism, and Robert Boyle gives this 'often try'd remedy for an ague: Boil yarrow in new milk, till it be tender enough for a cataplasm. Apply this to the patient's wrists, just when the cold fit is coming; and let it lie on till the fit is gone; and if another fit comes, use fresh cataplasms as before.'

Bibliography

Agrippa, Henry Cornelius, *Three Books of Occult Philosophy*. Llewellyn, St. Paul 1993.

Albertus, Frater, *The Alchemist's Handbook*, Weiser Books, San Francisco, first published 1974.

Atwood, Mary Anne, *A Suggestive Inquiry into Hermetic Mystery*. William Tate, Belfast 1920.

Banckes, Richard, *Banckes' Herball*, 1520.

Bartlett, Robert Allen, *Real Alchemy: A Primer of Practical Alchemy*. Ibis Press, USA 2009.
—— *The Way Of The Crucible*. Ibis Press, USA, 2009.

Black, William George, *Folk-Medicine: A Chapter in the History of Culture*. Elliot Stock for The Folk-lore Society, London 1883.

Bolnest, Edwardo, *Aurora Chymica or A Rational Way of Preparing Animals, Vegetables and Minerals For Physical Use*. Printed by Tho. Ratcliffe and Nat. Thompson, London 1672.

Chancellor, Philip M. (Compiled & edited by), *Handbook of Bach Flower Remedies*. C.W. Daniel Company, 1985.

Cockayne, Thomas Oswald (Collected & edited by), *Leechdoms, Wortcunning, and Starcraft of Early England*. Longman, Green, Reader and Dyer, London 1866.

Culpeper, Nicholas, *The Complete Herbal*. Thomas Kelly, London 1835.

Dalyell, John Graham, *The Darker Superstitions of Scotland*. Waugh and Innes, Edinburgh 1834.

Dubuis, Jean, *Philosophers of Nature: Spagyrics Vol. I & Vol. II*. Triad Publishing 1987.

Folkard, Richard, *Plant Lore, Legends and Lyrics*. Sampson Bow, Marston & Company, London 1892.

Fortune, Dion, *The Mystical Qabalah*. Society of the Inner Light, London 1998 (first published 1932).

Frazer, Sir James George, *The Golden Bough: A Study in Magic and Religion*. Abridged version, Macmillan & Co. London 1925.

French, John, *The Art of Distillation*. Richard Cotes, London 1651.

Friend, Rev. Hilderic, *Flowers and Flower Lore*. Swan Sonnenschein and Co. London, 1883.

Gerard, John, *The Herball or General History of Plants*. (*Gerard's Herbal*), Bracken Books, London 1985.

Glauber, Johann Rudolph (Trans. Chris. Packe), *A Spagyrical Pharmocopoea, Vol. I to VII*. RAMs Digital.

Grieves, Mrs, *A Modern Herbal*. First published 1931 by Jonathan Cape. Cresset Press, Britain 1994.

Hall, Manly P., *Man: The Grand Symbol of the Mysteries*. The Philosophical Research Society, USA 1947.
  —— *The Secret Teachings of All Ages*. Gerald Ducksworth & Co. Ltd, London 2006.

Hartmann, Franz, *Occult Science in Medicine*. Theosophical Publishing Society, London 1893.
  —— *Paracelsus*. Kegan Paul, Trench, Trubner, & Co. London 1896.

Hazelrigg, John (collated and rendered by), *The Book of Formulas*. The Hermetic Publishing Company, New York 1904.

Hollandus, Johann Isaac, *Medicinal Recipes From his Secrets Concerning Vegetall and Animal Work*, 1652. Translated from the German by Leone Miller, 1978. RAMs Digital.

Junius, Manfred P., *Spagyrics: The Alchemical Preparations of Medicinal Essences, Tinctures and Elixirs*. Inner Traditions, USA 1985.

Jung, Carl, *Alchemical Studies*. Translated by R.F.C. Hull, Routledge & Kegan Paul Ltd. London 1983.

Lévi, Eliphas, *The History of Magic*. Translated by A.E. Waite. Red Wheel/Weiser, USA, 2001.

Lisiewski, Joseph C., *Israel Regardie & the Philosopher's Stone*. Falcon Press, 2008.

Northcote, Lady Rosalind, *The Book of Herbs*. John Lane, London 1903.

Nottingham, Gary St. M., *Ars Spagyrica*. Mercurius Press.

Regardie, Israel, *Garden of Pomegrates*. Rider & Co. London, 1932.

Rohde, Eleanour Sinclair, *A Garden of Herbs*. Philip Lee Warner, London 1920.

Schulke, Daniel A., *Ars Philtron*. Xoanon Publishing, USA 2001.
—— *Viridarium Umbris*. Xoanon Publishing, USA 2005.

Stavish, Mark, *Practical Plant Alchemy*. Mark Stavish 1996.

Thiselton-Dyer, T.F., *The Folk-Lore of Plants*. Chatto & Windus, London 1889.

Waite, A. E. (edited by), *Collectanea Chemica*. Vincent Stuart Ltd., London, 1963.

Waite, A.E., *The Hermetic and Alchemical Writings of Paracelsus the Great*, (2 volumes). University Books Inc. New York 1967.

Wilde, Lady, *Ancient Legends, Mystic Charms, and Superstitions of Ireland*, Ticknor and Co., Boston 1887.